LAWYERS AND TH

For the 2010 Hamlyn Lectures, Alan Paterson explores different facets of three key institutions in a democracy: lawyers, access to justice and the judiciary. In the case of lawyers he asks whether professionalism is now in terminal decline. To examine access to justice, he discusses past and present crises in legal aid and potential endgames, and in relation to judges he examines possible mechanisms for enhancing judicial accountability. In demonstrating that the benign paternalism of lawyers in determining the public good with respect to such issues is no longer unchallenged, he argues that the future roles of lawyers, access to justice and the judiciary will emerge only from dialogues with other stakeholders claiming to speak for the public interest.

ALAN PATERSON is Professor of Law and Director of the Centre for Professional Legal Studies at Strathclyde University. He is also the Chair of the International Legal Aid Group. As research adviser to the Scottish Legal Aid Board he has been responsible for the training and monitoring aspects of the peer review programme of quality assurance for legal aid lawyers in Scotland. He served as a member of the Council of the Law Society of Scotland from 2000 to 2008, and of the Judicial Appointments Board for Scotland from 2002 to 2008. In 2008 he was appointed as an inaugural member of the Scottish Legal Complaints Commission, and in the following year he was awarded the OBE for services to legal education and the law.

LAWYERS AND THE PUBLIC GOOD

Democracy in Action?

ALAN PATERSON

CAMBRIDGE UNIVERSITY PRESS
Cambridge, New York, Melbourne, Madrid, Cape Town,
Singapore, São Paulo, Delhi, Tokyo, Mexico City

Cambridge University Press
The Edinburgh Building, Cambridge CB2 8RU, UK

Published in the United States of America by Cambridge University Press, New York

www.cambridge.org
Information on this title: www.cambridge.org/9781107012530

© Alan Paterson 2012

First published 2012

Printed in the United Kingdom at the University Press, Cambridge

A catalogue record for this publication is available from the British Library

ISBN 978-1-107-01253-0 Hardback
ISBN 978-1-107-62628-7 Paperback

To Michael

CONTENTS

TABLES

ILLUSTRATIONS

THE HAMLYN TRUST

The Hamlyn Trust owes its existence today to the will of the late Miss Emma Warburton Hamlyn of Torquay, who died in 1941 at the age of 80. She came of an old and well-known Devon family. Her father, William Bussell Hamlyn, practised in Torquay as a solicitor and J.P. for many years, and it seems likely that Miss Hamlyn founded the trust in his memory. Emma Hamlyn was a woman of strong character, intelligent and cultured, well-versed in literature, music and art, and a lover of her country. She travelled extensively in Europe and Egypt, and apparently took considerable interest in the law and ethnology of the countries and cultures that she visited. An account of Miss Hamlyn by Professor Chantal Stebbings of the University of Exeter (one of the Hamlyn trustees) may be found, under the title 'The Hamlyn Legacy', in volume 42 of the published lectures.

Miss Hamlyn bequeathed the residue of her estate on trust in terms which it seems were her own. The wording was thought to be vague, and the will was taken to the Chancery Division of the High Court, which in November 1948 approved a Scheme for the administration of the trust. Paragraph 3 of the Scheme, which follows Miss Hamlyn's own wording, is as follows:

> The object of the charity is the furtherance by lectures or otherwise among the Common People of the United

Kingdom of Great Britain and Northern Ireland of
the knowledge of the Comparative Jurisprudence and
Ethnology of the Chief European countries including the
United Kingdom, and the circumstances of the growth
of such jurisprudence to the Intent that the Common
People of the United Kingdom may realise the privileges
which in law and custom they enjoy in comparison with
other European Peoples and realising and appreciating
such privileges may recognise the responsibilities and
obligations attaching to them.

The Trustees are to include the Vice-Chancellor of the
University of Exeter, representatives of the Universities of
London, Leeds, Glasgow, Belfast and Wales, and persons co-
opted. At present there are eight Trustees

Professor N. Burrows, The University of Glasgow
Professor I.R. Davies, Swansea University
Ms Clare Dyer
Professor C. Stebbings [representing the Vice-Chancellor of
    the University of Exeter]
Professor R. Halson, University of Leeds
Professor J. Morison, Queen's University, Belfast
The Rt Hon. Lord Justice Sedley
Professor A. Sherr, Institute of Advanced Legal Studies,
    University of London (Chair)

From the outset it was decided that the objects of the Trust
could be best achieved by means of an annual course of public
lectures of outstanding interest and quality by eminent lectur-
ers, and by their subsequent publication and distribution to a

wider audience. The first of the Lectures were delivered by the Rt Hon. Lord Justice Denning (as he then was) in 1949. Since then there has been an unbroken series of annual Lectures published until 2005 by Sweet & Maxwell and from 2006 by Cambridge University Press. A complete list of the Lectures may be found on pages xv to xviii. In 2005 the Trustees decided to supplement the Lectures with an annual Hamlyn Seminar, normally held at the Institute of Advanced Legal Studies in the University of London, to mark the publication of the Lectures in printed book form. The Trustees have also, from time to time, provided financial support for a variety of projects which, in various ways, have disseminated knowledge or have promoted to a wider public understanding of the law.

This is the 62nd series of lectures which was delivered by Professor Alan Paterson in three different locations. The first took place at the Playfair Library Old College, University of Edinburgh on 1st December 2010. The second was due to be held at the McCance Lecture Theatre University of Strathclyde Glasgow on 7th December 2010. Snow closed the University and the whole of Glasgow on that day and the Lecture was postponed to 1st March 2011. The third lecture was held at the Beveridge Hall, Senate House, University of London on 14th December 2010 and was chaired by Lord Hope of Craighead, Deputy President of the Supreme Court. The Board of Trustees would like to record its appreciation to Professor Paterson himself and also to Edinburgh, Strathclyde and London Universities who generously hosted these Lectures. It was a good year for snow and each occasion brought some uncertainty about the weather. In true form the Hamlyn lecturer moved effortlessly around the nations both intellectually and geographically, coped with being snowed off and finishing late, bringing a new look at Lawyers and the Public Good.

December 2010, London
AVROM SHERR
Institute of Advanced Legal Studies
Chair of the Trustees

THE HAMLYN LECTURES

ACKNOWLEDGEMENTS

To be asked to deliver the Hamlyn Lectures is a major honour for any academic. To be asked as a Scots legal academic to deliver them is also a rare honour. Professor Sir Neil MacCormick experienced that honour before I did but due to illness was prevented from delivering his lectures. Lord Bingham of Cornhill did deliver his lectures but tragically also suffered an untimely death shortly thereafter. As will be clear from the text of my lectures I owed a significant debt to each of them. To Neil for supervising my doctoral thesis on the Law Lords forty years ago and to Tom for the insights which he afforded to me two years ago as to the role of the Law Lords in their final decade, when he was the presiding Law Lord.

I am greatly indebted to the Hamlyn Trustees for the invitation to deliver the 2010 lectures, to Professor Kim Economides, Chairman of the Trustees, who first brooked the topic and to Professor Avrom Sherr, his successor, who supported me throughout the eighteen months of roller-coaster preparation leading up to the lectures. I was exceedingly fortunate to follow so shortly in Professor Dame Hazel Genn's footsteps and to benefit from frequent discussions with her as to how best to meet the challenges entailed in the lectures. Nothing was too much trouble for her, whether it was the full text of her lectures and powerpoints or advice as to possible audiences for the lectures.

ACKNOWLEDGEMENTS

The first lecture was given in the Playfair Library, the jewel in the crown of the Old Quad, Edinburgh University where in the sixties I first studied law. Professor Douglas Brodie, Head of the Edinburgh Law School, was the generous host who secured the venue, funded the excellent dinner and proffered the assistance of Lorna Gallacher as a very efficient event organiser. The lecture was admirably chaired by Lord Hamilton, Lord President of the Court of Session. Pride of place, however, must go to the audience of eighty doughty individuals who braved the snow to join us on that occasion, being rewarded for their pains by one of the first showings of video extracts from the oral hearing in the *JFS* appeal before the Supreme Court.

The second lecture was meant to be at Strathclyde University a week later but this time the elements defeated the audience and it had to be postponed by several weeks. The second lecture in chronological terms therefore was in the Beveridge Hall, Senate House, the University of London, thanks to the efforts of Professor Avrom Sherr, Director of the Institute of Advanced Legal Studies and to his immensely helpful team of Eliza Boudier and Belinda Crothers. Lord Hope, the Deputy President of the Supreme Court and Chancellor of my own university, chaired the lecture with charm and insight and the splendid dinner was provided by the Hamlyn Trustees and Cambridge University Press.

The final lecture was delivered at the McCance Lecture Theatre, Strathclyde University, organised twice over by the ever patient and supportive Fiona Lynn and chaired by Professor Jim McDonald, the Principal of the University and the splendid host and provider of the subsequent dinner.

ACKNOWLEDGEMENTS

The key to the delivery of a major lecture series is the strength of the 'home team'. Here I was exceedingly fortunate to have the very generous support of my Head of School, Professor Mark Poustie, the help of our shared PA, Carol Hutton, and the invaluable assistance of the technical support team Craig Grant, David Sams and Sharon Ennis and of several very enthusiastic and diligent research assistants – Danielle McLaughlin, Darren Murdoch, Emma Boffey and Paul Ferrie. However, the strongest team needs an audience, and I was particularly touched at the number of friends, whether from near or far (the latter including Michael and Ruth Browde, Peter van den Biggelaar, Ulrike Schulz and Leny de Groot), colleagues and others who made the time to attend the lectures.

To turn three lectures into a coherent manuscript requires the input of many willing minds. To the admirable staff of Cambridge University Press, Finola O'Sullivan, Richard Woodham, Lyn Flight and Daniel Dunlavey the thanks of an over-anxious author are clearly due. To the Parliamentary Archives for permission to reproduce two photographs from the final year of the House of Lords Appellate Committee thanks are also due. In composing the text I have benefited immensely from the input of many individuals to different aspects of my thinking which has ultimately appeared in the book. In addition to Honours students and research interviewees (primarily Law Lords and counsel) too numerous to mention over the years, special thanks should go to Stephen Bailey, John Bell, Michael Browde, Brice Dickson, David Feldman, Hazel Genn, Tamara Goriely, William Holligan, Colin Lancaster, Kate Malleson, Neil McIntosh, Neil MacCormick, Lindsay Montgomery, Richard Moorhead, Chris Paterson, Russell

ACKNOWLEDGEMENTS

Pearce, Jenny Rowe, Avrom Sherr, Roger Smith, Richard Susskind, Adam Tomkins and Michael Zander.

Finally, I must thank my longsuffering family. My children, Christopher, Rachel and Michael, provided much needed therapy in frequent trips to London whilst Alison, my wife, not only attended all the lectures (as did my sister Jill and my friend Duncan) but coped with the stress associated with their preparation, delivery and publication with characteristic generosity of spirit.

July 2011, Glasgow
ALAN PATERSON
Strathclyde University

1

Introduction: determining the public good

Miss Hamlyn, a not particularly well to do but widely travelled spinster and daughter of an English solicitor, bequeathed the world a startling bequest – a bequest so far-sighted that her trustees immediately sought guidance as to whether it was void from uncertainty since the beneficiaries were that indeterminate category 'the Common people of this Country'. Fortunately for the legal world, counsel was of the opinion that this meant the UK public and the judge in Chancery, a mere six years later, agreed.[1] Bleak House this was not, however, since the capital of the trust remained largely intact. The novelty of the bequest was twofold. First, it was to fund public legal education – a concept which was not invented for another fifty years. Secondly, the lectures were *not* to instil in the public an awareness of their rights so much as to heighten their consciousness of the responsibilities and obligations imposed on them from living in a country that believed in the rule of law. I have no doubt therefore that Miss Hamlyn would have approved of 'Lawyers and the Public Good' as a title for the lectures – and also their iconoclastic theme – namely, that legal institutions are too important in a modern democracy to be left to lawyers alone.

---

[1] I am indebted to the *History of the Trust*, penned by Chantal Stebbings which appears on the Trust website.

But first a word of explanation. The honour of being only the second Scots academic to deliver these lectures (Professor Sir T. B. Smith was the first) should have fallen to Sir Neil MacCormick, but his untimely illness and death prevented this, and the mantle fell to me. I think I was Neil's first doctoral student, since in 1969 he became the co-supervisor of my D.Phil at Oxford. It was on the Law Lords – and partly at Neil's suggestion the Law Lords will feature strongly in my lecture on the judiciary. Neil shared my fascination in the process of judicial decision-making and was the ideal supervisor for a young person in need of confidence and reassurance whenever writers' block came to call. His enthusiastic optimism has stayed with me throughout my professional career.

In the lecture series I grappled with how to determine the public good – the best interests of the public[2] – in relation to three key institutions in a democracy: lawyers, access to justice and the judiciary. It follows that in the chapters to follow I will focus on different facets of lawyers, access to justice and the judiciary. In the case of lawyers, I shall be asking whether professionalism is now in terminal decline; for access to justice I will discuss the current crisis in legal aid and what or who will determine its future; and in relation to judges, I shall examine possible mechanisms for judicial accountability. I will argue that in the past lawyers and judges have

[2] For a discussion of possible meanings of the public good and the public interest see Legal Services Institute, *The Regulation of Legal Services* (London: College of Law, February 2011). For my purposes there is little difference between the two terms. They refer to 'that which is for the collective benefit of the whole community' as opposed to 'all consumers', 'minorities' or 'individuals' in society.

assumed that the determination of the public interest with respect to questions such as these has been for them to decide in a process of (usually) benign paternalism. In recent decades, however, these assumptions have come under challenge from other bodies claiming to represent the public interest with respect to legal institutions, such as the consumer movement, the competition authorities, regulators, politicians and the Government.

Taking first the legal profession and professionalism. From around the start of the twentieth century the solicitors' branch of the profession in England and Scotland had begun to see professionalism as akin to a tacit concordat with the state by which in return for high status, reasonable rewards, limited competition (including the monopolies) and self-regulation they would deliver expertise, a service ethic, access to legal services and public protection. As the century drew on, the clearer it became that the profession had had much the best of this 'bargain', and in the last thirty years the concordat has been re-negotiated at the hands of the state and the consumer movement in order to deliver more from the profession in pursuit of the public interest. The debates over alternative business structures (ABS) were but the latest manifestation of this, with the Scottish Bar (the Faculty of Advocates) spectacularly negotiating a deal whereby it was exempt from the reforms on public interest grounds, providing that it allowed free transfer between the status of advocate and that of solicitor advocate.

As for access to justice, from the earliest times the legal profession has set the terms of engagement. Its members have determined the nature and scope of the services that they were prepared to deliver to those of limited means,[3] and those that they were not.[4] For a long time they were successful throughout the United Kingdom in resisting or co-opting new modes of delivery (such as law centres), since it was they who determined what was in the public interest. Again, only in the last twenty years have dialogues with the state and the legal aid boards produced a publicly funded legal assistance market that owed as much to external stakeholders' views of the public interest as to those of the profession.

Finally, judicial independence and judicial accountability. Over the centuries, perhaps inevitably, the judiciary have placed the emphasis on the former rather than the latter, through their ability to determine what was in the public interest in their judgments and public pronouncements. The last decade, however, has seen a dialogue with the state and other stakeholders over issues such as complaints, discipline, training and appointment, in the shape of concordats.

It is easy to forget that these dialogues between the profession and the wider world in relation to each of these legal institutions are of comparatively modern origin. The result, as Miss Hamlyn would have understood, is that when it comes to legal professionalism, legal aid reform and judicial accountability others now have a role to play in determining the public interest. The days of legal paternalism have not come to an end, but they have, perhaps, begun to be numbered.

---

[3] Primarily assistance in the fields of crime, personal injury and family law.
[4] Typically social welfare law (including housing and debt).

2

Professionalism re-assessed: what now for lawyers?[1]

> This book is about a crisis in the American legal profession. Its message is that the profession now stands in danger of losing its soul.[2]

> For the first time in fifty years or more a real battle is being fought to determine who controls professions and professionals ... I refer to this struggle as a crisis in professionalism.[3]

> **The crisis of legal professionalism.** The future of professionalism in England and Wales is uncertain.[4]

In this chapter I will examine how and why professionalism in lawyers is said to be in decline, and in so doing I will explore the contemporary understanding of what it means to be a member of the profession for the twenty-first-century lawyer. And, for those impatient to get to the end, I shall conclude by arguing that, despite everything, professionalism has been,

---

[1] The original working title for this chapter was 'Whither the Legal Profession(s)?'. However, as one learned senator of the College of Justice remarked to me, 'don't you mean: "Whether the legal professions?"'. On reflection, he had a point.

[2] Anthony Kronman, *The Lost Lawyer* (Cambridge, MA: Harvard University Press, 1993), p. 1.

[3] Gerald Hanlon, *Lawyers, the State and the Market* (London: Macmillan, 1999), p. 1.

[4] Andrew Boon and Jennifer Levin, *The Ethics and Conduct of Lawyers in England and Wales*, 2nd edn (Oxford: Hart Publishing, 2008), p. 56.

and remains, a socially constructed concept that is the product of dialogues involving more than lawyers.

Solicitors: a profession in crisis?

Wherever you go in the English-speaking world, commentators have greeted the new millennium with the gloomy assertion that for lawyers the era of professionalism is in crisis, if not at an end. However, closer scrutiny of these jeremiads reveals that their apparent unity is indeed only apparent – they are not saying the same thing:

(1) At one end of the spectrum are the commentators, like Richard Susskind (though in fairness there is no one quite like Richard), who anticipate the possible demise of the profession itself and presumably professionalism with it. His latest book, *The End of Lawyers?*, focuses on the inevitability of an increasing commoditisation of the work of lawyers and with it a degree of de-professionalisation, but adds somewhat ominously, 'For those lawyers who cannot [adapt] … I certainly do predict that their days are numbered … The market … will increasingly drive out … outdated lawyers.'[5]

(2) At the opposite end of the spectrum is a critique that paradoxically is a product of the continued success of professions. Its complaint is that the coinage of 'profession and professional' is being debased, since there are

[5] Oxford University Press, 2008, p. 3. In fairness to Susskind he sees the decline in lawyers as being concentrated among those involved in routine and repetitive work that can be done by others.

more professions than ever, at least 130 at the last count according to the Panel on Fair Access to the Professions report,[6] and allegedly one in three of the current workforce is now in a professional or managerial job. After all, if we are all professionals now, then in the words of Gilbert and Sullivan, 'when everyone is somebody, then no one's anybody'.[7] If successful, this usage will mark the death of professionalism in an exclusive sense,[8] ironically thereby removing part of the cachet responsible for the rampant pursuit of professional status in the last century. It is as though the older meaning of a professional – 'a member of learned vocation' – has been replaced by a newer one – 'one who earns a living from an occupation as opposed to the amateur who does it on an unpaid basis'. A similar, but less obvious, dilution of the meaning of 'professional' can be seen in descriptions of behaviour as 'unprofessional', for example, habitually turning up to work late, or not taking a 'professional' pride in what one does, in one's appearance, courtesy or personal hygiene. In these contexts 'professional' has not lost all of its content of being 'a good thing', since it contains an explicit reference to standards, but such a usage strips out much of

---

[6] Panel on Fair Access to the Professions, *Unleashing Aspiration* (London: Institute of Career Guidance, Cabinet Office), p. 14, available at: www.icg-uk.org/article607.html.

[7] Act 2, 'The Gondoliers'.

[8] See Herbert Kritzer, 'The Professions are Dead, Long live the Professions: Legal Practice in a Post Professional World', *Law and Society Review*, 33 (1999), 713.

the other content from the term that once distinguished certain occupations from others.[9]

(3) The rising numbers of lawyers has troubled other commentators and, indeed, doubtless existing practitioners who fear that it will lead to an over-supply of lawyers, a decline in profitability, a shortage of work and ultimately the decline of the profession. Rick Abel, the foremost thinker on the legal profession in the Anglo-American world in recent times, of course, viewed the dramatic increase in UK lawyers over the last twenty-five years as a loss of market control by the occupation[10] – in his eyes the death of professionalism as we know it.

(4) The expansion of the profession has been accompanied by an ever increasing specialisation within the profession,[11] and with it a diversification of work settings. The traditional image of the lawyer as an independent practitioner has given way to a world in which the significant majority of lawyers now work either as employees in larger law firms or as in-house lawyers.[12] This dramatic shift

---

[9] For a slightly different take on definitions of professions and professionalism see Kritzer, 'The Professions are Dead'.

[10] R. Abel, 'The Decline of Professionalism', *Modern Law Review*, 49 (1986), 1; R. Abel, *English Lawyers between Market and State* (Oxford University Press, 2003), p. 475.

[11] See Richard Moorhead on specialisation, 'Lawyer Specialization – Managing the Professional Paradox', *Law and Policy*, 32 (2010), 226.

[12] Some critics have asserted that this development has undermined the independence and autonomy of the profession, a view that has received support from the ruling in the European Court in the *Akzo* case, denying the clients of in-house lawyers the right to legal professional privilege. A variant on this critique can be found in the writings of those

stimulated the 'death of the profession' doom-smiths to posit the replacement of a collegiate model of the profession with a factionalised, heterogeneous and fragmented, but curiously non-diverse model.[13]

(5) Perhaps the most sustained critique of today's profession, however, relates to the twin threats posed by consumerism and commercialism[14] as the deregulation of the legal services market which began over twenty years ago steamrollers on. Anthony Kronman, the Dean of Yale Law School, is but one of several contemporary commentators to claim that the modern profession has lost its traditional ideals, its public spiritedness and its moral compass as our opening quote revealed. The fear is that

lamenting the impact of the 'new managerialism' on the professional autonomy of NHS doctors or legal aid lawyers. See, e.g., Hilary Sommerlad, 'Managerialism and the Legal Profession', *International Journal of the Legal Profession*, 2 (1995), 159; Simon Caulkin, 'Are the Real Pros being Managed out of Existence?', *The Observer*, June 2006; Hanlon, *Lawyers, the State and the Market*.

[13] See R. Nelson *et al.*, *Lawyers' Ideals/Lawyers' Practices: Transformations in the American Legal Profession* (New York: Cornell University Press, 1992).

[14] See e.g., 'In the Spirit of Public Service', Report of the American Bar Association's Commission on Professionalism (Chicago, IL: American Bar Association, 1986) and the swathe of commentaries that it spawned. The ABA has returned to the topic of the decline in professionalism again and again, see Dane Ciolino, 'Redefining Professionalism as Seeking', *Loyola Law Review* 49 (2003), 229. The threat from commercialism is not new, however, as Justice Brandeis observed in 1905: 'Able lawyers have become adjuncts of great corporations and have neglected to use their powers for the protection of the people.' From the speech 'Opportunity in the Law', to the Harvard Ethical Society in 1905.

when consumerism forced open Pandora's de-regulatory box what flew out was not sin, but one deadly sin in particular: greed.

What are we to make of such divergent diagnoses, apart perhaps from concluding that professionalism is a 'feel good' concept that everyone can sign up to as a 'good thing', even though not everyone may understand the concept in quite the same way? As the eminent professional ethicist Deborah Rhode put it in 2001, 'I have long argued that a central part of the "professionalism problem" is a lack of consensus about what exactly the problem is, let alone how best to address it.'[15] Certainly, a great deal of effort has been devoted to trying, and failing, to reach some kind of agreement as to what the concepts mean. Part of the problem stems from the fact that, 'profession' and 'professionalism' have a range of meanings and usages that bedevil easy analysis.[16] However, this in turn reflects the fact that they are social constructs whose meaning has varied over time, and inevitably reflect the social and economic context of the time. The vision of a homogeneous occupation with consensual values serving as a bulwark between the individual and the state clearly emanated from the post-war era, while the heterogeneous, factionalised body with divergent ethics was as clearly a 1960s stereotype. Again,

---

[15] Deborah Rhode, 'Professionalism', *South Carolina Law Review*, 52 (2001), 458 at 459. See also Deborah Rhode, 'The Professionalism Problem', *William & Mary Law Review*, 39 (1998), 283.

[16] This is as true in the medical world as with lawyers. See, e.g., Delese Wear and Julie Aultman (eds.), *Professionalism in Medicine: Critical Perspectives* (New York: Springer, 2006).

the professional project to control the market coincided with public disillusion with the over-controlling professionals of modernity. Post-modern thinking, on the other hand, sees only a fragmentation of the legal professions into competing sub-professions,[17] while in today's post-professional era the commentators only see crises.[18]

Where do I stand? Let me return to the challenge of commercialism. Some observers believe that lawyers in the large city law firms are really little different from ordinary businesspersons, that they have more in common with their corporate clients than with sole practitioners specialising in criminal legal aid. This line of thinking has received support in recent times from an unexpected quarter: the ranks of American writers on professional ethics. They have witnessed with bemusement and irritation the American Bar Association (ABA) thrashing about as it grappled with a perceived decline in professionalism in lawyers over the last thirty years – a perception also held by the ABA's medical counterpart. A series of Commissions into professionalism have produced little more than platitudes and a yearning for a golden age of professionalism, which somehow is always located ten years earlier than anyone on the Commission can remember, and is largely apocryphal. What has troubled the ABA has been the way in which the focus on the bottom line is consuming more and more of the waking hours of today's legal professional. They attribute this to a decline in professional standards, following

---

[17] A. Boon et al., 'Postmodern Professions?', Journal of Law and Society, 32 (2005), 473.
[18] Kritzer, 'The Professions are Dead'.

the de-regulation of the legal services market in the last thirty years. The ethicists think that the ABA have got it all wrong: lawyers have always been entrepreneurial and money-oriented. Instead of taking pleasure from their achievements, however, they are being made to feel guilty for being financially successful. The ethicists' answer is to decry all talk of legal professionals as being more high-minded than businesspersons and to urge the abandonment of the false dichotomy between being a businessperson and a professional. All of which is fairly redolent of the alternative business structure (ABS) debate in the United Kingdom in recent years. The school of thought that we are all businesspersons now, talks up the excellence of business education, the ubiquitousness of consumerism and its adjunct goal of excellence in service provision, the rise of business ethics and of corporate social responsibility. In sum, to these critics there is now little point in distinguishing between professions and businesses. Put at its starkest, there is no difference between lawyers and plumbers. Both have the skills and competencies that their clients lack – both therefore benefit from information asymmetry and the client's need for trust. Both have a college training, both are required to pass tests, both are highly paid, both invest in continuing professional development and both are needed to sort out society's dirty work. So does it all boil down to the greater self-conceit of the lawyers? The Department of Constitutional Affairs minister[19] who observed that she couldn't see why consumers should not be able to obtain legal services as easily as they could buy a tin of beans, presumably thought so. In my view that is to miss

[19] Bridget Prentice, quoted in *The Telegraph*, 18 October 2005.

some obvious truths. Lawyers are expected to adhere to the core professional values of independence, loyalty, confidentiality, upholding the rule of law and their duties to the court – plumbers are not. Today's lawyers are expected to do *pro bono* work and to have a service ethic – plumbers are not. Finally, lawyers are required to carry not only indemnity insurance, but also to underwrite the honesty of their competitors in the shape of client security or guarantee funds – a point that has caused some friction with the imminent arrival of ABSs – plumbers are not.

Frankly, I do not find the attempts to ameliorate the demise of professionalism through emphasising the ethical nature of modern businesses very convincing. The scandal of Enron and the devastation to world economies triggered by greedy bankers do not make happy exemplars for the new business paradigm. Whatever the attractions to some of supermarkets entering the legal services markets, we should be wary of the comforting, generic blandness of supermarkets blinding us to their ability to be ruthless when they feel the necessity (Figure 2.1).[20] When the credit crunch hit, it is alleged that one of the supermarket chains informed its specialist architects[21] that they would accept an immediate cut of 40 per cent in their fee rates, otherwise the client would go elsewhere.

Nevertheless, I agree with the new critics on one point. It is not uncommon for commentators to write as though professionalism – the essence of being a professional – is

---

[20] Cf. recent accusations of attempts collectively to hold down milk prices or to impact on property prices in town centres.
[21] Whose sole specialism related to designing supermarkets.

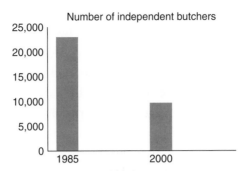

Figure 2.1   Supermarket effects on the High Street
Source: A. Simms *et al.*, *Ghost Town Britain, the Threat from Economic Globalisation to Livelihoods, Liberty and Local Economic Reform*, The New Economics Foundation, 2002, p. 12.

synonymous with altruistic or 'other related' professional attributes and values such as:

expertise;
access;
service ethic;
public protection –
    ethical codes and the core values;
    ombudsmen/complaints commissions;
    client security/guarantee fund/indemnity insurance.

However, such a view risks perpetuating the false dichotomy between being a profession and being a business, which has rightly been criticised by American commentators[22] and City

---

[22]   See, e.g., Russell Pearce, 'How Law Firms can do Good while Doing Well (and the Answer is Not Pro Bono)', *Fordham Urban Law Journal, Symposium on Professional Challenges in Large-Firm Practice*, 33 (2005), 221.

14

firms alike. As I have argued elsewhere,[23] in my view professionalism involves a combination of the other related attributes I have just cited, on the one hand, and a range of largely self-oriented attributes, on the other (Table 2.1). I accept therefore that professionalism is a Janus-faced concept: with the profession and the professional required to manage the tension between self-interest and other related values, between benefits and obligations, for this model works at the level of the profession and of the individual professional. This is a dialectical tension, but it is, I believe, a healthy and normal feature of professional life in the twenty-first century. Just as the Law Society of Scotland is required by section 1 of the Solicitors (Scotland) Act 1980 to promote the interests of the solicitors' profession and the interests of the public in relation to that profession, so the individual professional has to balance his or her own interest against the best interests of the client. A medical sociologist recently observed that the central paradox in medicine is the 'tension between self-interest and altruism'.[24] He could equally well have been discussing the legal world. The tension has been dubbed by American ethicists as *relational self-interest*. On this view it has always been in the public interest for lawyers to make a reasonable living in return for serving their clients and the wider community.[25] If you like, the status and rewards

---

[23] See, e.g., A. Paterson, 'Professionalism and the Legal Services Market', *International Journal of Legal Studies*, 3 (1996), 137 and A. Paterson, 'Self-Regulation and the Future of the Profession', in D. Hayton (ed.), *Laws Future* (Oxford: Hart Publishing, 2000).

[24] Cited in J. Coulehan, 'You say Self-interest, I say Altruism', in D. Wear *et al.* (eds.), *Professionalism in Medicine* (New York: Springer, 2006), p. 124.

[25] See G. Beaton, *Why Professionalism is still Relevant* (2010), available at: au.linkedin.com/in/georgerbeaton.

Table 2.1 *The nature of professionalism*

Professionalism	
Obligations	*Benefits*
Expertise	Status
Access	Reasonable rewards
Service	Restricted competition
Public protection	Autonomy

Source: A. Paterson, 'Professionalism and the Legal Services Market', 1996.

on the right of the model stem from the expert knowledge on the left being applied in the interest of the client and the collective client: namely, the public interest. Again the independence said to be vital to a profession is needed to protect the client as well as the profession. It follows that I do not accept that professionalism is best conceived of as the left-hand side of the diagram alone: it is both parts and the tension between them.

The renegotiation of professionalism

Clearly this has resonances with the social bargain view of professions espoused by the functionalists of the 1950s, but there are key differences, which is why I call it 'neo-contractualism'. To me it is more of a contract than a bargain – the model makes no assumptions as to the fairness or otherwise of the tacit compact – but it does posit that the concept of professionalism, being socially constructed, is a dynamic one which therefore evolves over time. Indeed, that is just what the compact has been doing in the last thirty years. What was seen as the traditional concept of professionalism survived relatively unchanging from the 1930s to the 1980s – long enough for everyone to forget that it had ever been different – but it began to be re-negotiated following the de-regulation of the 1980s and 1990s. Just as in the medical profession, lawyers had concentrated too much on defining the client's or patient's needs and to what extent they would be met rather than focusing on the client/patient expectations. In the late twentieth century, this degree of paternalism was unacceptable; the more so since it went hand-in-glove with a failure of the professions to deliver on their side of the bargain.[26] Crudely speaking, the re-negotiation took the form of a strengthening of the elements on the left-hand side of the model and a weakening of those on the right-hand side, because the impetus for change came from an unlikely alliance between then Prime Minister Margaret Thatcher and the consumer movement. Some commentators saw it as the demise of professionalism, but like the late lamented Cyril Glasser[27] I believe that what we are seeing is only the end of an outdated view of professionalism, not the concept of professionalism itself.

In the remainder of this chapter I will look at the post-ABS dialogues which will help to dictate what any new form of professionalism will look like,[28] and I will take each element in

---

[26] For a neo-contractualist analysis of the medical profession see R. Rosen and S. Dewar, 'On Being a Doctor', A King's Fund Discussion paper (London, 2004).

[27] See C. Glasser, 'The Legal Profession in the 1990s', *Legal Studies* 10 (1990), 1 at 10.

[28] Other believers in a new professionalism include Glasser, Kritzer, Halliday and Moore.

professionalism in turn to examine how it is withstanding the challenges from commercialism and consumerism.

Status

High status was part of the professional project in England and Wales for solicitors – to enable them to catch up with the Bar. Although they were successful, the growth in the number of professions in the last fifty years, as referred to earlier, has probably reduced the cachet associated with being a profession. There is some UK survey evidence to suggest that the approval ratings for lawyers have declined in the last decade,[29] and it is certainly arguable that in post-modern society respect for authority figures such as professionals has declined. However, the MORI annual 'Trust in Professions' poll does not suggest that trust in the learned professions has greatly changed in the last twenty years. Moreover, the ratings for lawyers far outstrip those for business executives. As against that, high-profile scandals, such as the recent miners' compensation cases in England and Wales will not have helped. The spread in anti-lawyer jokes is sometimes said to epitomise the fall in solicitors' status, but lawyers are probably the most avid tellers of such jokes. Despite scrutiny by academic researchers (there are two scholarly books about anti-lawyer jokes),[30] it is

---

[29] Ipsos MORI 2006. For a discussion drawing on the concerns of several professions at the declining public esteem for professionals see SPADA, *British Professions Today: the State of the Sector* (London: SPADA, 2009).

[30] See M. Galanter, *Lowering the Bar, Lawyer Jokes and Legal Culture* (Madison, WI: University of Wisconsin Press, 2005) and Y. Ross, *The Jokes on Lawyers* (Sydney: Federation Press, 1996).

unclear that the prevalence of such jokes (over a million on Google apparently) is a sound indicator of a significant loss of social status for the profession.[31]

Reasonable rewards

Although the Law Society of Scotland has conducted an annual cost of time survey for many years using external experts, obtaining accurate figures for the earnings of lawyers in the United Kingdom has never been easy. Forty years' experience of lawyers in the United Kingdom tells me, however, that they will rarely admit that business is good even when it becomes abundantly clear a few years later that business was booming at that time. They are somewhat quicker to complain that times are hard. In the past fifteen years, legal aid lawyers in particular have complained that they are underpaid. Certainly, they are not being paid at private rates, whereas sixty years ago legal aid lawyers were paid 90 per cent of private rates. However, one of the problems of information asymmetry is that in the personal services market, market forces do not work effectively to keep price rises down. As late as 1997 the legal aid rate was 85 per cent of the judicial rate allowed to be recovered in non-legal aid cases. However, lobbying from the Law Society in relation to the judicial rate over the subsequent few years meant that by 2002 the legal aid rate was only 52 per cent of the

---

[31] My favourite remains the one about scientists replacing rats with lawyers in their experiments. First, rats are smarter than lawyers, second, you can get fond of rats and, third, there are some things that a rat won't do.

permitted judicial rate.[32] The profession therefore contributed to its own dissatisfaction with legal aid rates, leading some to cease doing legal aid work.

A further quirk about feeing systems is that they all contain perverse incentives. To safeguard against this, professional ethics requires that fees must be fair and reasonable in all the circumstances, and in fiduciary law the fee must be one that an independent lawyer would regard as fair and reasonable. In England and Wales, the Law Society has long offered an independent fee assessment service. The Law Society of Scotland has never offered such a service, but clients can generally insist[33] that their bill is checked by an auditor who is independent of the legal profession to ensure that it is fair and reasonable. Unfortunately, as the Scottish Executive's Research Working Group on Competition in the Legal Services Market reported in 2006, this consumer protection measure has occasionally been subverted in situations where the relationship between the auditor and the instructing solicitor has become too close.[34] This problem was adverted to again by the outgoing Accountant of Court in an unpublished report in 2010

---

[32] See Annex 1, *Report by the Research Working Group on Competition in the Legal Services Market in Scotland* (Edinburgh: Scottish Executive, 2006), p. 154.

[33] Provided they have not signed a 'written fee charging agreement' with the lawyer agreeing the solicitor's remuneration, which has the effect of excluding independent auditing. Nonetheless, it remains the case that the fee must not be grossly excessive and that it must be fair and reasonable in the circumstances. See A. Paterson and B. Ritchie, *Law, Practice and Conduct for Solicitors* (Edinburgh: W. Green, 2006), ch. 10.

[34] See Research Working Group Report, para. 10.200.

but, as of the time of writing, the Scottish Government seems unconvinced of the need for action. Certainly, the Scottish Government response to the Gill Report, announced on 11 November 2010, indicates that they believe that the problems of auditing can be dealt with by further training. I fear that this limited response may be insufficient to ensure that the Scottish auditing system for non-court fees is fit for purpose or adequate to protect the public interest.

Solicitors benefit not just from fees. They also benefit from the interest they can earn on the clients' money that they hold. When the sums are large and held for a substantial period lawyers have always remitted the interest to the client on straightforward agency principles. But in other cases where the sums were smaller or retained for a short period, in the past solicitors in the United Kingdom normally simply hung on to it. This was a curious reading of the law of agency and not one that was shared in the United States, Canada, Australia and the Commonwealth. In these countries the interest earned on clients' money was used for worthy causes such as legal education, law libraries or the funding of legal aid cases. It took a decision of the House of Lords in the 1960s in the Scottish Appeal, *Brown* v. *Inland Revenue* [35] to establish what every first-year law student should have known: namely, that the money did not belong to the law firms. The law societies swiftly passed practice rules setting the parameters as to when the interest should be paid to the client, but these were drawn up in pre-computer days. Now, it would be perfectly feasible to allocate all the interest earned by one client to that

[35] *Brown* v. *Inland Revenue* 1964 SC (HL) 180.

client. However, as we shall see in Chapter 3, the Ministry of Justice is casting envious eyes on the money. Unfortunately, with interest rates the way they are, whatever the Treasury does is not likely to generate very much by way of funding the public good. In fact, the very variability of interest rates coupled with the true ownership of the interest convinces me that we should simply return it to the client.

Of course, many firms have suffered with the recession, staff have had to be laid off, recruitment of new entrants curtailed and cash flow closely watched. Indeed, income targets have become the bane of many a lawyer's existence. It was cash flow which eventually drove Halliwells – a significantly sized English firm – under, but there were elements of greed also. Certainly, it looked suspiciously like crocodile tears when a few large City firms drastically reduced their employee bonuses for public relations reasons – granting a windfall increase to their partners' profits – which had remained remarkably stable in any event.

Restraints on competition and market control

All of the major restraints on competition within the profession have come under sustained scrutiny in the last thirty years. Fixed fees to prevent price cutting have been abolished, the ban on advertising lifted and the monopolies of the profession including those in relation to conveyancing for gain, elements of probate or executry work and rights of audience in the higher courts have all been eroded in both England and Scotland. The ban on fee-sharing with unqualified persons will be the next restraint to go, since it is that rule that prevented the formation of ABS and the payment of referral fees. The former as is well known allows non-lawyers, such as banks, insurance companies, supermarkets and hedge funds, to own and control English law firms in their entirety and up to 49 per cent of the capital of Scottish law firms, leaving the remaining 51 per cent in the hands of lawyers and 'other regulated professionals', whoever they may be. At one time it was thought that this might include any professional grouping from hairdressers to ballet dancers, however, the consultation by the Scottish Government in 2011 as to the breadth of 'other regulated professionals' suggests that they have a narrower concept in mind. Referral fees entail a third party referring cases to a lawyer in return for a fee. Such fees have been a source of ongoing tension in England and Wales, with research conducted in 2010 under the auspices of the Legal Services Board (LSB) and the Legal Services Consumer Panel (LSCP) appearing to suggest that even fees of £900 for a personal injury referral can be paid with no one experiencing any downsides.[36] This smacks of the logic of alchemy, although we have yet to hear the last word on the subject. In Scotland we have yet to hear the *first* word on the subject. In all the ABS debate in Scotland, no one seems to have devoted any attention to the payment of referral fees which will be permitted with the arrival of ABSs. In England and Wales, there is a code of practice insisting that clients are made aware of referral fees from the outset. The LSB and the

---

[36] Legal Services Board, 'Referral Fees, Referral Arrangements and Fee Sharing', Discussion Document (London, September 2010), para. 1.13, available at: www.legalservicesboard.org.uk/what_we_do/pdf/20100929_referral_fees.pdf.

LSCP research reveals that this requirement is being more honoured in the breach than the observance. We have been warned.

Numbers: market control on supply of producers

Market control theorists such as Abel asserted the demise of professionalism because the profession ceded control of the number of entrants to the profession to the universities. But how many lawyers is too many lawyers? That sounds like the beginning of another anti-lawyer joke. Yet it is a serious question. The ratio of lawyers per head of the population varies around the world. In Scotland we have 1.4 private practice solicitors per 1,000 of the population[37] and 3.2 doctors per 1,000 of the population. Lawyers are not always portrayed in the media as acting in the public good and, corporate clients apart, legal services are often a distress purchase. So what does the public interest say about the number of lawyers that is healthy for a society to have? More to the point, who will decide what is in the public interest in this area? The Government? The profession? The judiciary? The universities? None of them: it should be the public in the shape of the market. Workforce planning is notoriously difficult, and if the medical world with all its government resources can get it dramatically wrong as seems likely to be the case with a *surplus* of over 1,000 hospital and community specialty doctors and around 600 GPs predicted for Scotland

---

[37] The comparative figure in England and Wales is 1.6 solicitors, in the United States it is 3.2, in Spain it is 1.5 and in Brazil it is 2.8.

in 2014,[38] why should the lawyers expect to do any better. Stephen Mayson is one commentator who asserts[39] that there are many more lawyers in England and Wales than are required. However, part of that argument turns on assumptions as to what it is reasonable to expect lawyers to do.

I do think that expectations play a part here. The broader one's conception of the role of lawyers in society the less concern one will have over numbers. The work done by Scottish lawyers 200 years ago was far broader in scope than it is today, since they were also bankers, insurers and accountants as well as lawyers. Alternative business structures will force us to embrace a more entrepreneurial vision of the future role of the lawyer. Part of the answer to the numbers question relates to expectations for earnings of new entrants to the profession as to what they should be earning as lawyers when they are thirty. There are clear signs today that if entrants to the profession expect too much by way of early return, then more senior partners will choose the less expensive specialist paralegal in place of the greater all-round promise of the new entrant. Susskind's latent legal market may be colonised by new business units with fewer lawyers and many paralegals as the work grows ever more commoditised. One alternative, which might actually fit quite well with the latest plans for repaying student fees, would be to create jobs for young lawyers whose salary

---

[38] Reshaping Medical Workforce Project Board, *Consultation on Speciality Training Numbers from 2011 to 2015* (Edinburgh: Scottish Executive, 2010).

[39] In his inaugural lecture, 'Legal Services Reforms', at the College of Law on 21 March 2007, and again in interview with Jonathan Ames, 'Is there Work for so Many Solicitors?', *The Times*, 24 March 2011, p. 59.

at thirty-five does not exceed £30,000. In a very real sense tomorrow's youth may have to choose between being a specialist paralegal or a slightly more expensive lawyer generalist, particularly in the field of poverty legal services.

In the last two years some in the profession (the Chairman of the English Bar was among the most recent)[40] have complained about the number of law graduates being produced by UK law schools. The implicit suggestion is that the latter should have anticipated the credit crunch when the profession did not. I do not think that law schools will reduce their intakes – in part because they rightly believe that law is a good general education for many careers. Nor do I think that the profession – however tempting it may be – should seek to interfere with the market by endeavouring to restrict entry to the profession. Down that route looms the Office of Fair Trading. Moreover, Richard Moorhead's blog in 2010 contained some fascinating figures showing that for the last fifteen years the market has kept the number of traineeships and LPC (Diploma) graduates in England and Wales in remarkable proximity (Figure 2.2). However, I do think that the profession and the law schools should be working together more closely and that had they done so there would have been more understanding of each other's position.

My own view is that in Scotland we have too many law schools for a small country and that we should have fewer, larger, but better resourced law schools.[41] Most law schools in the

---

[40] See his speech to the annual Bar conference, P. Lodder QC, 'Raising the Bar', 25th Annual Bar Conference, 6 November 2010.

[41] Which was why Strathclyde and Glasgow universities worked together for a decade in the shape of the Glasgow Graduate School of Law. It

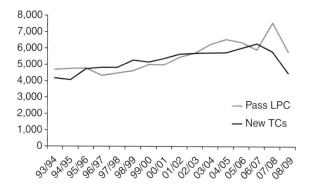

Figure 2.2   Legal Practice Certificate holders and Training
Contract numbers
Source: http://lawyerwatch.wordpress.com, 2010.

United Kingdom have suffered from under-funding over the
years because their undergraduate students attract the low-
est unit of resource in academia. Why that should be so is a
long story, but part of it stems from the fact that the era when
a majority of entrants to the profession took a full-time university law degree began less than fifty years ago. By the time
the full-time LLB came to Scotland in 1961 it was too late to
argue for special treatment from the funding councils. While
the City Solicitors Educational Trust has invested considerable
sums in legal education and academic posts in England and
Wales, there has been no equivalent for Scottish law schools.
Efforts over the last thirty years to persuade Scottish law firms
to sponsor posts or developments in Scottish law schools have
rarely been very successful, in part because partnerships (and

may have come to an end recently, but the thinking behind it remains as
valid today as a decade ago.

the way they are taxed) are not geared to investments, and alumni giving in the United Kingdom lags far behind that in the United States. That said, I do not regard the Scottish profession's unwillingness to invest in the future of the profession as a healthy sign. In my view Edmund Burke was right to claim that society owes a debt to the past and a duty to the future, and it holds equally true of the legal profession. Ironically, had the profession invested more in the law schools, student fees and the future of the profession, the partnership between the profession and the law schools that is seen at its best in the Diploma in Legal Practice or the Legal Practice course, would have been much closer and to the benefit of both. For a variety of reasons the relationship between the legal profession and academe[42] has never been as close or as mutually beneficial as in the field of medicine. Some of us regret this and therefore welcome the recent strengthening of the relationship through the Joint Standing Committee on Legal Education for Scotland.

Regulation and autonomy

Although the attempt to control the market was a key part of the professional project and of traditional professionalism, independence and self-regulation were almost as important to the profession. Today, pure examples of self-regulation have largely disappeared from the professional map, although the Faculty of Advocates has held on to it for longer than most. Its

[42] See F. Cownie and R. Cocks, *A Great and Noble Occupation* (Oxford: Hart Publishing, 2009).

decline came about because it came to be seen as an anachronism – 'chaps regulating chaps' as the CEO of the English Legal Services Board dubbed it in 2009[43] – and because economists argued that it could be a cloak for rent-seeking, for regulatory capture, ineffective disciplinary procedures and anti-competitive practices.[44] Market failure on this scale was assisted by the degree of information asymmetry between lawyers and all but the most sophisticated of their business clients. The response of governments, consumer organisations and competition authorities around the world has been uniformly to move away from self-regulation[45] towards co-regulation – a

[43] Chris Kenny, 'The Paradoxes of Regulatory Reform', Oxford/Harvard Legal Symposium, 11 September 2009, p. 8. See LSB website at: www.legalservicesboard.org.uk.

[44] These arguments can be found in writings such as A. Ogus, *Regulation: Legal Form and Economic Theory* (Oxford: Hart Publishing, 2004), p. 108; M. Seneviratne, *The Legal Profession: Regulation and the Consumer* (London: Sweet & Maxwell, 1999), pp. 28–9; and D. Rhode, 'Policing the Professional Monopoly', *Stanford Law Review*, 34 (1981), 1.

[45] Exceptionally fragmented markets for legal services, a greatly enhanced tension between commercial pressures and professional integrity, and continuing debates as to whether regulation is standing in the way of new business structures and external investment have led the EU, other states, legal professions and societies to re-consider the regulatory framework for the profession and other providers of legal services in a wide range of jurisdictions. Explicit reviews of self-regulation and the profession have recently occurred in Australia (Victoria – twice, New South Wales and Queensland), New Zealand, the EU, Ireland, Scotland and England and Wales. For academic discussions of regulation and the legal profession in Australia, see C. Parker, 'Competing Images of the Legal Profession: Competing Regulatory Strategies', *International Journal of the Sociology of Law*, 25 (1997), 385; C. Parker, 'Law Deregulation via Business Deregulation', *International Journal of the Legal Profession*, 6 (1999), 175; and C. Parker, *Just Lawyers* (Oxford University Press, 1999).

combination of self-regulation and external regulation – or even beyond. This has tended to complicate matters, prompting Ann Abraham, the English Legal Services Ombudsman, to memorably label it as a 'regulatory maze',[46] a description widely popularised by Sir David Clementi, author of the famous Clementi Report[47] on the Regulatory Framework for the Legal Profession in 2004. Certainly, the haphazard evolution of co-regulation has led to inefficiencies, which in turn has led some critics to push for purely external or independent regulation like the General Medical Council (GMC) or the Legal Services Board. Personally, I think we have been too quick to write off co-regulation. The next step after ineffective co-regulation should have been to try effective co-regulation (that is, a partnership model of regulation between the profession and external stakeholders, in pursuit of the public interest) rather than to leap ahead to independent regulation.

As for the future, the advent of ABS will bring with it entity regulation: akin to regulating and disciplining firms

For Canada, see H. W. Arthurs, 'The Dead Parrot: Does Professional Self-regulation Exhibit Vital Signs?', *Alberta Law Review*, 33 (1995), 800 and W. H. Hurlburt, *The Self-Regulation of the Legal Profession in Canada and in England and Wales* (Edmonton, Alberta: Law Society of Alberta and Alberta Law Reform Institute, 2000). For a more recent take on the regulation of legal services see Legal Services Board, *Understanding the Economic Rationale for Legal Services Regulation – A Collection of Essays* (London: Legal Service Board, 2011).

[46] Legal Services Ombudsman, *Annual Report, 2001–2002* (London: Stationery Office, 2002).

[47] D. Clementi, *Review of the Regulatory Framework for Legal Services in England and Wales*. Final report (London: Ministry of Justice, December 2004).

rather than individual practitioners, which hitherto has been the norm in most, but not all, jurisdictions.[48] This will have complexities, since complaints will also continue to be raised against individuals within the firms.[49] The impact of entity-based regulation on the ethics of corporate lawyers has been questioned[50] – but the regulators of New South Wales and Queensland are convinced that proactive entity regulation not only works well, but that it can even reduce the number of complaints.[51] I am less convinced by the concomitant move in England and Wales to principle-based regulation.[52] This is the form of regulation that was less than spectacularly successful in policing bankers before the credit crunch. Re-branding 'light-touch' regulation as 'risk-based' regulation looks a little like the triumph of hope over experience. To abandon the

---

[48] In Victoria, Australia (Legal Practice Act 1996, s. 137) firms can be guilty of professional misconduct. Moreover, in relation to inadequate professional services, conflict of interest and money-laundering penalties can be imposed on the firm as well as individual lawyers.

[49] Where the individuals are from different professions this risks the perplexing outcome for complainers that the same behaviour by different professionals working together may attract quite different responses from their respective professional bodies because of differences in the ethical standards of each profession.

[50] See Joan Loughrey, *Corporate Lawyers and Corporate Governance: International Corporate Law and Financial Market Regulation* (Cambridge University Press, 2011) for a trenchant argument to this effect.

[51] See Steve Marks, 'Views from an Australian Regulator', *Journal of the Professional Lawyer* 2009, 45.

[52] Known also as outcomes focused regulation by the Legal Services Board and the Solicitors Regulatory Agency. See SRA, *Achieving the Right Outcomes* (January 2010).

Solicitors Code of Conduct 2007 – itself a radical departure from the *Guide to the Professional Conduct of Solicitors*, which had taken several years of effort to devise – within three years, seems somewhat regrettable. Particularly since the leading expert on principle-based regulation, Professor Julia Black of the LSE, has indicated that the new general principles that are being brought in will not be able to form the basis for disciplinary prosecutions without detailed rules being drafted as an overlay to the new principles. She has also observed that OFR/PBR can work only if there is a high degree of mutual trust between the regulated and the range of new regulators, which may be a big ask.[53] I think the Scots are right to be wary of embracing principle-based regulation, although ironically the Law Society of Scotland's Standards of Conduct are very close in content and structure to the principles proposed by the Solicitors Regulatory Agency (SRA) south of the border. Of course, the City firms are expecting their own form of risk-based regulation irrespective of whether they embrace external ownership – they made that much clear to the Hunt and Smedley regulation reviews and, as so often nowadays, they got their way. Light-touch regulation must not be allowed to get in the way of profit maximisation. It all depends on who defines the risk. The City firms and the regulator see it as a risk to the corporate client. Others think there may be more risk to the public good *from* the corporate clients assisted by their legal advisers. Certainly, we should bear in mind the wry

---

[53] Seminar on the Future of Legal Services organised by the Legal Services Board at SOAS, 14 June 2010.

observation of Lord Hunt,[54] echoed by Lord Neuberger,[55] that the 'principles-based approach does not work with individuals who have no principles'.

One other trend that I consider to be misconceived is that currently espoused by the consumer movement and governments in England and Scotland and endorsed by the Clementi Report: namely, the push for the representative and regulatory functions of the profession to be split. This has taken place in England and has not been an obvious success. Moreover, it risks introducing into the legal arena the medical model of the Royal colleges, the British Medical Association and the GMC, which has not been successful either. Over the years doctors have come to see the representative bodies as their leaders, not the regulatory body. But talk to any doctor and it is clear that financial prosperity and dissipated regulation has not improved job satisfaction. Splitting the functions encourages the professional association to become like a trade union focusing largely on their members' interests rather than having to wrestle with the dualism of safeguarding the public good as well as the profession's good at one and the same time, which as I indicated at the outset is the essence of professionalism. Strange to say, section 1 of the Solicitors (Scotland) Act 1980, which famously includes an obligation on the Law Society to promote (a) the interests of the solicitors' profession in Scotland and (b) the interests of the public in relation

[54] Lord Hunt, *Legal Services Regulation Review* (London: Law Society, 2009), p. 38.
[55] Speech by Lord Neuberger, 'The Ethics of Professionalism in the Twenty-first Century', 23 February 2010.

to that profession in Scotland, got it right. Equally interestingly, when in June 2010 three segments within the profession sought to take over the representative role for the profession leaving the Law Society solely concerned with regulation, the proposal was defeated comprehensively in a referendum with 73 per cent of the 4,138 members who voted opting for the Law Society to retain both functions.[56] These forces are inevitably in tension from time to time, but the solution is not to sacrifice the interests of the client to the interests of the lawyer or vice versa. Rather, it is to recognise that the tension is a healthy and normal dialogue and to live with the challenge of keeping the forces in balance.

To recap: I argued at the outset that professionalism was a Janus-faced, socially constructed concept that resembled a pact between the profession and the community. I argued further that this concordat has been re-negotiated over the last thirty years in part because the state and the consumer movement considered that the profession was not delivering on its side of the bargain. What were the attributes on the public's (or the client's) side of the concordat? Expertise, access, a service ethic and public protection.

Expertise

Expertise or specialist knowledge is a given – unless it exists there is no information asymmetry to justify the regulatory

---

[56] This has not prevented the proponents of separation from continuing to lobby for a change, ostensibly in the name of the public interest, although more cynical voices have observed that the change would also benefit financially some of the organisations pushing for the reform.

bargain. Mandatory CPD came some time ago, but since then there has been relatively little progress. Equally surprising in its own way is the position over specialisation. Both in England and Scotland the degree of *de facto* specialisation by solicitors has increased dramatically in the last thirty years, resulting in the present-day situation where at least 70 per cent of solicitors in mainland United Kingdom describe themselves as specialists. However, the accreditation of specialists by the law societies has not kept pace with these developments.[57] The Writers to the Signet, sensing an opportunity, have launched their own accreditation programme, benefiting in part from work done with the Glasgow Graduate School of Law, but we are a far cry from the fellowship examinations of the medical profession. The Royal Colleges of Physicians alone recognise twenty-six medical specialities, with a further ten specialities in surgery. Each of these specialisms has its own standards and examinations. Why have lawyers not felt it necessary or desirable to develop in the same way? Currently, once a solicitor has completed his or her two-year traineeship they are considered by the Law Society to be qualified to practice in any area of law – provided they do not do so on their own. One's suspicion is that this situation cannot last and that if there is, as seems possible, an attempt to remove the reserved areas or legal monopolies of the legal profession, we will then see a more rigorous assessment process for specialists emerging, as the profession responds in an effort to preserve the brand of solicitor.

[57] See Richard Moorhead, 'Lawyer Specialisation – Managing the Professional Paradox', Cardiff Law School Research Paper No. 5, 2008, see n 11, above.

The position in relation to quality assurance in the profession has been more auspicious.[58] Large law firms have been using file review to quality-assure their work as a standard part of risk management for some time in order to meet the demands of professional indemnity insurers providing additional top up cover for the firms. Legal aid firms in England, Wales and Scotland have also been subject to a rigorous peer review of their files for over seven years. This is a little heralded success story for the profession, since they have been slow to publicise that the results of this independent audit have shown that the overwhelming majority of legal aid lawyers deliver a good quality service to their clients. Indeed, the Scots peer review programme has been demonstrated in several foreign jurisdictions and taken up by notaries in the Netherlands as well as by a range of private law firms in that country. In future, as the solicitor brand comes under increasing pressure from other legal services providers it is possible that peer review could extend to the whole profession to form a part of the next significant initiative on the public's side of the concordat: namely, regular re-validation of practitioners. Doctors in the United Kingdom, in the aftermath of Shipman, have already been planning for some time to introduce a regular re-validation programme. A GMC consultation on this reported in October 2010 and the great majority of respondents were in favour. Initial pilots in England were somewhat over-ambitious, but it seems likely that re-validation throughout the

---

[58] See, however, the Legal Services Consumer Panel, *Quality in Legal Services* (London, November, 2010) which called for quality assurance to spread to all firms.

United Kingdom will include elements of CPD, appraisal and performance review. Some may think that this is a foible of the medics which will pass the lawyers by, but I do not think so. The consumer society will expect the legal profession – if it survives as a distinct entity – to go down this route of travel. The Thomson review of higher Rights of Audience in Scotland recommended in 2010 that there should be re-certification for all Scots pleaders on a five-year cycle, and the English Bar has accepted that five-yearly re-accreditation should be introduced for criminal advocates under the Quality Assurance for Advocates scheme.[59] A similar proposal has been floated by the Chair of the Legal Services Consumer Panel in England for all lawyers, and was endorsed in the Panel's recent paper on *Quality in Legal Services*.[60] The Panel were particularly influenced by the research report, which they had commissioned, that showed that consumers assume that the regulators are *already* quality-assuring all lawyers on a regular basis.

Access

This I understand to mean the obligation on the profession to provide access to the legal system that they have done so much to create and maintain. Lawyers are the gatekeepers to our legal system, as Kafka's bitingly satirical account in *The Trial*[61] reminds us. Suffice it to say that I believe that part of

---

[59] C. Baksi, 'Neuberger Endorses Accreditation Scheme', *Law Society Gazette* 10 November 2010.

[60] Baksi, 'Neuberger Endorses Accreditation Scheme'.

[61] F. Kafka, *The Trial* (London: Penguin Books, 1994).

professionalism is the onus placed on the profession to assist those who lack the funds to enable them to gain access to the courts. As Dame Margaret Bazley put it in her recent stunning report on legal aid in New Zealand, 'Lawyers belong to a profession. With the status of that profession goes obligations. One of those obligations is to enhance access to justice for people who would otherwise find it difficult to access legal services.'[62] The duty to act *pro bono publico* is one that is rightly coming back into fashion in Scotland, influenced in part by the better organised programmes in England and the championing of the Lord Advocate Elish Angiolini. For centuries the profession in the United Kingdom provided poverty legal services to the indigent through noblesse oblige – or as senior partners put it to young apprentices, *our* noblesse, *your* oblige. Indeed, as late as the 1960s the great bulk of senior lawyers in Edinburgh, whether in litigation firms or at the Bar, had spent part of their youth attending the Edinburgh Legal Dispensary, which until recently operated in the Old Quad of the University.

There is another sense of access which hitherto has not been seen as playing a large part in the definition of professionalism: namely, equality of access to the profession itself.[63] In both England and Scotland approximately 46 per cent of those solicitors in private practice are female. However, the gap between the proportion of female entrants to the profession

---

[62] Dame Margaret Bazley, *Transforming the Legal Aid System* (Wellington: Ministry of Justice, 2009) p. 74.

[63] In 2010 Hector Macqueen provided a most stimulating account of 'Scotland's First Female Law Graduates', available at: http://womeninlaw. law.ed.ac.uk/documents/WilsonLecture.pdf.

in the last thirty years and the proportion achieving partnerships and the upper reaches of the profession is large and, dis-
turbingly, is becoming larger (Figures 2.3 and 2.4). The same
can be said for ethnic minorities or those from lower income
backgrounds. Given the regulatory objective of a more diverse
profession in the Legal Services Acts it may be that this is an
issue that regulators will be required to address in the future.
I am told that there have been improvements on the work–
life balance front in the large law firms – if so, it is not before
time – but we should be seeing it in job-sharing and the balance of the partnership.

Service ethic

To say that there is still a service ethic in professionalism today
is sometimes seen as more controversial than I believe that it
actually is. What I have in mind here is not some vague assertion that being a professional entails a form of altruism in
which the interests of society or the public – the generalised
other – must be put before those of the lawyer. In this sense,
the rhetoric of the past is not helpful because it has led us to
a situation where in law, as in medicine, altruism instead of
being empowering has become suspect.[64] This is neither historically accurate nor normatively plausible. Rather, I wish to
focus on the continuing tension between public interest and
client interest in the lawyer's role. Kronman railed against the

---

[64] See Fred Hafferty, 'Measuring Professionalism: A Commentary', in
David Stern (ed.), *Measuring Medical Professionalism* (Oxford University
Press, 2006), p. 281 at 295.

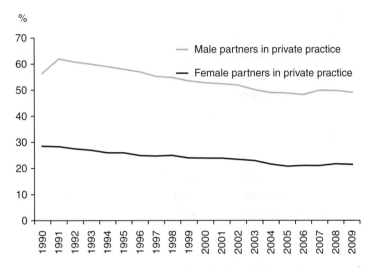

Figure 2.3   Partners in England and Wales by gender
Source: Law Society of England and Wales.

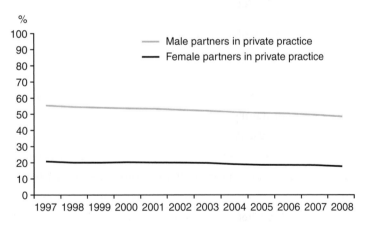

Figure 2.4   Partners in Scotland by gender
Source: Law Society of Scotland.

decline in the lawyer as statesman and in public service by lawyers, but the service ethic can be seen in other ways – *pro bono*
is but one of these. Lawyers today remain committed to the
service of their clients, what is at stake is whether lawyers are
also committed to serving a wider public interest. The regulatory objectives of the Legal Services Acts in both England and
Scotland certainly seem to require them to be so in the shape
of support for the rule of law and access to justice. I am in the
excellent company of Cyril Glasser[65] in believing and hoping
that they are, both in the guise of support for the rule of law
and access to justice, and also in a growing awareness that lawyers have duties to others than their clients and the court, an
issue to which I shall shortly turn.

Public protection

This element in professionalism has been one of the most
dynamic in recent years. Here the dialogue with non-lawyers
has been at its most active. Co-regulation and external regulation comes with significant, if not majority, lay participation,
whether on regulatory bodies, complaints committees or disciplinary tribunals. As each new code of conduct emerges,
so the pressure increases for consultation with external bodies.[66] The pro-active entity regulation required of ABSs will

[65] Glasser, 'The Legal Profession in the 1990s'. Faced by a diversity of work
setting, 'a common public service ideal, however ridiculous such a
notion appears, may be the cement which binds the profession together
and gives it a coherence which will enable it to survive', pp. 10–11.

[66] The Scots Standards of Conduct and Service of 2008 were the product of
consultation with consumer groups. The SRA has consulted widely as to

undoubtedly also require a dialogue with more than the legal community.

Frontiers of lawyer liability to third parties: extending the public interest

Lawyers have always owed ethical duties to the court and the justice system, but for centuries it was believed that their legal obligations were confined to their clients.[67] Gradually, however, the consumer society has forced the law to develop in this area. It all began with the snail in a bottle case, *Donoghue* v. *Stevenson*,[68] arguably Scotland's biggest contribution to international jurisprudence on liability to others. Over the last century there has been a trend to extend the legal obligations of lawyers beyond their liability to their clients[69] to a range of other persons who might be affected by their acts or omissions, including disappointed beneficiaries where a solicitor has negligently drafted a will.[70]

In the parallel territory of complaints against solicitors the battlegrounds are somewhat similar. In the last thirty years the hired-gun model of the lawyer has come under increasing attack by scholars,[71] though less so where there is

its new Handbook of Standards, *The Architecture of Change Part 2* and the Legal Services Consumer Panel was also involved.

[67] *Batchelor* v. *Patterson and Mackersy* (1876) 3 R. 914.

[68] 1932 SC (HL) 31.

[69] Primarily in contract but also in delict, confidentiality and fiduciary law.

[70] See *White* v. *Jones* [1995] 2 AC 207 and *Holmes* v. *Bank of Scotland* 2002 SLT 544.

[71] See D. Nicolson and J. Webb, *Professional Legal Ethics* (Oxford University Press, 1999) and the references contained therein. However,

an imbalance of power between the parties or where the client is particularly vulnerable. This reduction in strength of focus on client autonomy and the concomitant expansion in the duty of care to others – witnesses and even the other party – represents a re-writing of the contract between lawyer and client following on the re-writing of the professional contract with society. Today's regulators of the profession are even now grappling with what looks suspiciously like an ethic of care. We can see this in relation to third-party service complaints. As is widely known, lawyers in the United Kingdom have for more than a decade been required by statute to deliver an adequate professional service to their clients, failing which they can be required to pay compensation.[72] However, can a third party complain about the service provided by the other side's lawyer to their own client? The legislation seems to suggest they can, but it is unclear what the limits are. The issue has come up where a lawyer is instructed to write a solicitor's letter in trenchant and threatening terms to the other side. Are there any limits on the allegations and threats the lawyer can make? Does it make a difference if the letter defames the other side? Does it depend if the solicitor makes it clear that he or she is writing on the client's instructions? What if the lawyer accuses the other party of lying but doesn't use

---

for two recent works defending the traditional amoral role of the lawyer see T. Dare, *The Counsel of Rogues? A Defence of the Standard Conception of the Lawyer's Role* (Aldershot: Ashgate, 2009) and D. Markovits, *A Modern Legal Ethics* (Princeton University Press, 2010).

[72] In the last two years this liability has been extended from poor service to professional negligence.

the formula 'I am instructed to say that you are a liar'? Does it matter if the other side is unrepresented or vulnerable through age or infirmity? When, if ever, does the lawyer have to check the truth of what his or her client has told him? Does it matter if the story seems inherently implausible from the word go? We know that lawyers who raise court actions without checking their facts risk being accused of abuse of court and a wasted costs order, but can a duty to investigate arise at an earlier stage? Optimistic lawyers will tell you that the answer to all of these questions is 'No', and will point to the recent majority decision of the Inner House in *Law Society* v. *SLCC*.[73] I am not so sanguine. The majority in that case gave very little authority for their propositions and showed limited awareness that the world of the lawyer is changing. The criticism of counsel for the accused in the Milly Dowler trial in 2011 for his treatment of the victim's family in the witness box, is a clear portent that even in criminal cases adversarial advocacy has its limits.

Counsel

How do Advocates fit with the neo-contractual model? Surprisingly well is the answer. The negotiations over ABS are but the most recent example. Having failed to resist the reforms to the complaints system contained in the Legal Profession and Legal Aid (Scotland) Act 2007, the Faculty were determined to resist the introduction of partnerships

[73] [2010] ScotCS CSIH 79; 2011 SLT 31.

between advocates or between advocates and solicitors. On paper this was a difficult ask. The English Bar had not wanted to permit such partnerships or ABS either, but were unsuccessful in their efforts to resist the Government's and the Office of Fair Trading's (OFT) reforms. However, the Faculty had the advantages that come from a small jurisdiction. They were armed with research by an economist, Professor Frank Stephen, which showed that the library-based, central service model of operation with its low overheads was very efficient in economic terms and that provided there was free movement between the status of advocate and solicitor advocate, the competition objectives of the OFT would largely be met. With only 460 practising members they were able to argue that such partnerships and the conflicts of interest that would accompany them would be likely to greatly reduce the choice of advocates available to the litigants. In short, that an independent referral Bar was a public good. Accordingly, the Faculty reached a concordat with the Scottish Government exempting them from the de-regulation provisions of the Legal Services Bill. In return, however, the Faculty agreed that if partnerships with advocates were to remain off-limits, then transfer between the status of advocate and solicitor advocate would have to become little more than signing forms. This is a clear example of neo-contractual behaviour – even down to the Government failing to reduce the agreement to writing – a matter which is already having ramifications, as memories fade as to what was actually agreed.

In terms of public protection, the Bar in the United Kingdom has also been forced to give ground to consumerism, first, in the shape of ineffective assistance of counsel, then by professional negligence extending to what they do in court (except in criminal cases in Scotland),[74] and then by the extension of inadequate professional service (IPS) and unsatisfactory professional conduct to advocates and barristers. As yet the Scots advocates have not been found liable in expenses for raising groundless actions – although, as I have argued elsewhere,[75] I believe that the courts have the residual authority to make such a ruling without an equivalent of the statutory intervention covering wasted costs orders that exists in England and Wales.

The Faculty retains more of the trappings of traditional professionalism than solicitors. It is also more collegiate – indeed, it has sometimes been compared with an elite club – with its own quirks and rituals. One example is the Parliament House walk in the ancient Hall of the first Scots Parliament.

> This is the *Salle des pas perdus* of the Scottish Bar. Here by ferocious custom idle youths promenade from ten till two. From end to end, singly or in pairs or trios, the gowns and wigs go back and forward … Intelligent men have been walking here daily for ten or twenty years without a rag of business or a shilling of reward. In process of time, they may perhaps be made the Sheriff-Substitute and Fountain of Justice at Lerwick or Tobermory … to do this day after day and year after year, may seem so small a thing to the

[74] *Wright* v. *Paton Farrell* 2006 SLT 269.

[75] Paterson and Ritchie, *Law, Practice & Conduct for Solicitors*, para. 14.05.04.

inexperienced! But those who have made the experiment are of a different way of thinking, and count it the most arduous form of idleness.[76]

The question that troubles the informed layperson, how-ever, is whether the split between solicitors and counsel is in the public interest, or simply a device to boost legal fees. It is a debate which has rumbled on for over a century in the United Kingdom. The tide for the fusion of the two branches of the profession has ebbed and flowed several times in that period. There is no consensus among informed observers of the scene. Some in England think that the Bar in England and Wales will shrink to the Chancery Bar and Planning and the rest will merge with solicitors and ABS to a New Zealand style unification of the two branches of the profession. In Scotland, Ken Prichard, former Secretary of the Law Society of Scotland, and Len Murray, a Glasgow solicitor who was one of the most respected court pleaders of his generation, argued[77] that the split in the Scottish profession should rather be between the chamber practitioner and the pleader – the same division as exists in Europe – which would entail all court practitioners fusing into a single branch of the profession – which doubtless was the direction of travel implicit in the Thomson review in 2009.[78] I have no fresh insights on the issue, although forty years studying the legal profession in Scotland has taught me

[76] Robert Louis Stevenson, *Edinburgh: Picturesque Notes* (Edinburgh, 1879), pp. 21–2.
[77] In his autobiography, Len Murray, *The Pleader* (Edinburgh: Mainstream Publishing, 2002), p. 64.
[78] For a fascinating insight into contemporary thinking as to the possibilities of fusion in Scotland see the respondents reported in Emma

never to underestimate the power of the Faculty of Advocates to resist change it dislikes.

What of expertise, the core of counsel's claim to be a separate legal profession? Quality assurance will come whether through the Quality Assurance for Advocates scheme for assessing criminal advocates in England and Wales,[79] or re-validation or peer review for advocates and barristers doing legal aid work.[80] Even advocates now assert that they have become specialists – if not in certain areas of law, at least in the art of advocacy. But how effective is oral advocacy? Stories abound of cases won or lost at the trial level through asking the right or the wrong question in cross-examination.[81] But surely at the highest level the intelligence of the justices in the Supreme Court is such that advocacy does not make much difference there. When I first looked at appellate advocacy in the Lords thirty-five or more years ago[82] as a tyro D.Phil student at Oxford with Neil MacCormick and Philip Lewis as my supervisors, I concluded on the basis of interviews with Law Lords and counsel (sixty-one in all) that the oral dialogue between the Law Lords and counsel played a vital role

Boffey's enterprising 2010 Honours Dissertation, *Raising the Bar: The Impact of Solicitor Advocates in Scotland* (available from Strathclyde University Law School).

[79] See the Legal Services Commission, 'Quality Assurance for Advocates', (Discussion Paper February 2010), available at: www.legalservices.gov. uk/docs/cds_main/QAADiscussionPaper_Feb2010.pdf.

[80] *The Thomson Review: Rights of Audience in the Supreme Courts in Scotland*, April 2011, available at: www.scotland.gov.uk/Publications/201 0/03/15112328/0.

[81] See Murray, *The Pleader*, p. 146.

[82] A. Paterson, *The Law Lords* (London: Macmillan, 1982).

in decision-making in that court. Over the last two years, with the generous help of the Nuffield Foundation, I have interviewed a wide range of Law Lords, Lord Justices, senior counsel and others (forty-five in all) with a view to understanding judicial decision-making in the House of Lords in its final iteration. Once again I enquired into the importance of advocacy in relation to decision-making.

Slightly to my surprise, a number of the counsel whom I interviewed this time round were sceptical as to how often advocacy had a determinative effect on the eventual outcome of appeals in the Lords. As Jonathan Sumption QC said:

> I think that advocacy matters much more in perceiving what are likely to be regarded as the meritorious points, what are likely to be regarded as the direction the Lords will want to move in, than in actually the analysis of case law or statutes … I don't think it ever makes the difference between success and failure but I think it makes a difference to the reasoning of a decision, which can be in the public interest … I have found myself quite often reformulating the way that the issue is argued, not fundamentally, it's not jettisoning the grounds below, but trying to suggest a completely different approach to the problem. I think that's part of the function of counsel and I think it's an exercise which can make a considerable difference to the quality of the reasoning. Most judges start from the answer and work backwards. The House of Lords do that even more often than other courts. I think that it is quite unusual to shift the majority of the House from an opinion that they have initially formed. It happens but it's not that common, what you can shift is the reasoning.

These relatively modest assessments by counsel of what advocacy could achieve in the Lords might, if they were the whole story, make clients wonder why they pay out sometimes in excess of £20,000 a day for the QC of their choice. Fortunately, the Law Lords were in general rather more positive as to the impact of good advocacy. All the Law Lords told me that they had changed their mind during the oral argument, and not that infrequently, in some cases. This was true thirty-five years ago and remains true today. Lord Bingham was characteristically balanced and concise, 'In some cases certainly, but not all', before going on to observe of oral advocacy:

> There are some cases where I think the truth is that by the time everybody has read two judgments below and two quite lengthy Cases they've formed a view one way or the other and they don't change it. But, I think there are quite a lot of cases in which people read one Case and they think that's very persuasive and then they read the other and they think that's very persuasive and so they do genuinely go into court with open minds looking to counsel to try and get an answer. Not only does it vary, as you would expect, from case to case but it varies from individual to individual because I think some people reach much firmer opinions early on than others do.

I have published elsewhere examples of cases in the last twenty years where advocacy from counsel is thought to have swayed either the swing voter in a 3:2 case or sometimes the bulk of the court,[83] but the most spectacular of these was

[83] A. Paterson, 'Does Advocacy Matter in the Lords?', in J. Lee (ed.), *From House of Lords to Supreme Court* (Oxford: Hart Publishing, 2011), ch. 12.

undoubtedly in the *Chagos Islands* case.[84] This is the case which featured strongly in Neil MacCormick's valedictory lecture, and it was not a decision of which he approved. It should frankly have been an unwinable case for the Government. Between 1965 and 1973 the British Government had ruthlessly (and deceitfully, so that it did not reach the ears of the UN) expelled the indigenous inhabitants from the Chagos Islands to secure the principal island, Diego Garcia, as a military base for the United States. There was another island that might have done, but it had rare turtles on it which were considered less expendable than the Chagos islanders, whom the Government regarded as 'extremely unsophisticated'. The Government's tactics to persuade Mauritius to take the islanders were not exactly sophisticated themselves, however, as this conversation between a Colonial Office official and Mauritius politician reveals:[85]

> Look, old chap, you have a problem and we have a problem. Our problem is that the Americans want the population of the Chagos Islands removed, and we need somewhere to put them. Your problem is that you don't yet know what system of government you're going to get.
>
> Now, you have a choice. You can be sensible and take the Chagos Islanders, and we'll give you some money to help. In that case you can have a first-past-the-post electoral system and you'll be prime minister for ever. Or you

---

[84] *Bancoult v. Secretary of State for Foreign and Commonwealth Affairs* [2008] UKHL 61.

[85] Cited by Sir Stephen Sedley, 'The Long Sleep', in M. Andenas and D. Fairgrieve (eds.), *Tom Bingham and the Transformation of the Law* (Oxford University Press, 2009), p. 183.

can be difficult and refuse to take them, in which case
we'll give you proportional representation, and nobody
will ever be able to form a stable government. It's a matter
entirely for you.

Under challenge, Robin Cook, the then Foreign Secretary,
announced in 2000 that the islanders would be permitted to
return home to the islands, except Diego Garcia. However, in
2004 the Government changed its policy and without con-
sulting the islanders or Parliament covertly passed two orders
removing the islanders' right of abode in the islands and dis-
entitling them from returning without permission, which
would not be forthcoming. The validity of the orders was
challenged by the redoubtable Bancoult and he was successful before the Divisional Court and the Court of Appeal. The
Secretary of State in a seemingly desperate last throw, brought
in new senior counsel and appealed to the House of Lords.
The odds did not look good. The Government's position was
morally indefensible; Lord Bingham, no supporter of governmental misbehaviour, was in the Chair; the Press favoured the
underdog; and latter was represented by the doyen of appellate
advocates, Sir Sydney Kentridge. After a four-day hearing in
July 2008 and a delay of 111 days the judgment of the court was
handed down in the chamber of House of Lords on 22 October
2008. The Secretary of State had won by 3:2. How are we to
account for this? There was an element of luck. First, one of the
original Law Lords assigned to the hearing pulled out and he
was thought to have favoured the islanders, while his replacement did not. Secondly, Lord Bingham, unusually, did not get
his judgment out immediately because the long vacation and
his retirement intervened, whereas Lord Hoffmann did, which

helped to shore up the majority. However, the principal reason for the Government's surprising success was because their new senior counsel, Jonathan Crow QC, took a completely different tack in his printed argument. He took on the weak point in his case – the moral indefensibility of the Government's behaviour – by admitting it, but showing that the subsequent decision in 2004, after a review, of not to allow the islanders to return, although unpopular, was a rational policy to adopt because the infrastructural costs of making life on the islands supportable in the long run would be enormous. Expert advocacy had made the difference.

Conclusion

To sum up. In my view, what has been happening in the last thirty years is neither the death of professionalism nor of the profession, but the replacement of an outmoded model of professionalism.[86] Neo-contractualism accepts not only the dynamic nature of professionalism, but also its Janus-faced character and that the profession cannot expect largely to determine the content of the tacit compact with the public in the way that it was able to in the era of traditional professionalism between the mid 1930s and the mid 1980s. Increasingly, the public, directly and indirectly, have insisted on the renegotiation of the traditional model. If the profession held the whip hand in defining the public interest in relation to

---

[86] Cf. Cyril Glasser, 'Viewed in this sense, it is possible to argue that Professor Abel has merely been describing the ending of only one outdated type of professionalism, not the concept of professionalism itself,' in 'The Legal Profession in the 1990s', p. 10.

traditional professionalism, in the last thirty years, as I have endeavoured to show in this chapter, the balance has begun to be redressed. As Sellar and Yeatman[87] would say, this has been a good thing. Professionalism is too important to be left to lawyers alone to determine. It has been good for the public as they have received a better service from more competently trained lawyers, better protection from fraud and negligence and better compensation through IPS where the service has been deficient. Moreover, client-centred lawyering has moved from being a fringe pursuit of clinical legal education to a mainstream activity. On the other hand, it has also been good for the profession. Traditional professionalism made the profession complacent and uncompetitive, ensuring the continuation of the sorry trend whereby Scots lawyers gave up market after market that had once been theirs. Originally, the bankers, insurers, accountants, actuaries and estate agents of Scotland our lawyers gave up every one of these markets except the last, and they lost half of that. Not a moment too soon the profession has had to become more entrepreneurial and ABS will provide a further impetus to that trend. New ways of working are emerging: City firms are outsourcing work to India or unbundling the elements in a transaction that do not require an expensive lawyer. Susskind's predictions on commoditisation of routine legal work seem to be all too accurate. In truth, however, lawyers have quite a bit to go in terms of being better businesspersons. More should be doing MBAs. The typical business model for small- and medium-sized firms involves a

---

[87] W. C. Sellar and R. J. Yeatman, *1066 and All that* (London: Methuen, 1930).

dependence on overdrafts rather than interim feeing for work in progress. Cash flow, cash flow, cash flow should be printed on every fee-earner's desk.

It is not only their business skills that lawyers need to improve; the peer review of all of Scotland's legal aid lawyers on the civil side in the last few years has demonstrated that there is a need for better client care. Lawyers, like doctors, need to improve their client communication skills. Re-validation or re-accreditation will help here, since client satisfaction will form part of this. Finally, lawyers need better training in professional ethics to assist them in marrying the professional and business elements of their role.

But where is professionalism headed? As a dynamic concept we know that it will continue to evolve, but in what directions? Of the multiple possible parallel futures let me select four:

(1) The triumph of commercialism. In this scenario, the American ethicists whom I quoted earlier will be proved right in the end. Our efforts at reform will resemble the deck chairs on a well-known vessel. The core values will be further watered down and solicitors, or those in the large firms at least, will be indistinguishable from pure businesses.

(2) Professionalism as a compact will break down and be replaced by Kritzer's post-professionalism, where almost everyone is a professional and the solicitor's profession is an anaemic and nostalgic shadow of its former glory. The remaining vestiges of self-regulation will go, as will what is left of the professional monopolies. The focus of

the regulators will shift from lawyers to regulating a field of activity. The residual differences between legal services providers will shrink – certainly there will be a level playing field as far as regulation goes – there will be no distortions caused by differentiated regulatory costs, the same standards, processes and protections will apply to all providers of legal services.[88] Professionalism would be attenuated to what is in the objectives of the Legal Services Act. Were that to happen it is unclear who in England and Wales would have the role of supporting the rule of law and providing the legitimating role for the legal system. In Scotland that role would probably fall to the Faculty of Advocates.

(3) The profession will fragment and with it strong notions of professionalism. Large law firms will go in one direction, solicitor advocates in another and personal service firms in a third. The Law Society would be replaced by a range of membership bodies, rather as the Writers to the Signet, the Glasgow Bar Association and the Society of Law Agents hoped in the summer of 2010.

(4) My final scenario is that the reserved areas will remain with modifications as other groups such as confirmation agents and will-writers come into the fold. Differentiated regulation would also remain, with the not-for-profit sector and other providers regulated to the same minimum standards of competence as the professions but not in the same way. Professional conduct, IPS, the Master Policy

---

[88] See, e.g., Russell Pearce, 'The Professionalism Paradigm Shift', *New York University Law Review* 70 (1995), 1229.

and the Guarantee Fund would apply most rigorously to the professions, but their added regulatory burden would be justified by the commercial advantages arising from the cachet of profession and the brand of advocate or solicitor in particular. Just as advocates have sought to differentiate themselves from solicitor advocates – before ABS got in the way – so solicitors will turn to peer review and serious specialist accreditation to preserve the brand name. This need not lead to fragmentation – the medical profession has managed to remain remarkably united despite the many sub-specialisms that now exist among them.

It is not possible to say which of these futures is the most likely to eventuate – possibly some combination of the four – but I have little doubt that the approach of the large law firms will be crucial. Their influence in Government circles in England and Scotland was responsible for the advent of ABS, and they have the clout to call the shots on a wide range of fronts from training to regulation. This is not altogether a comforting thought. The behaviour of City firms over the conflict of interest rules has been unedifying[89] (a criticism which

[89] After sustained lobbying they persuaded the Law Society to allow acting in conflict situations, with informed consent. Within six months they were back saying it wasn't enough. Some of their clients might be difficult, so would the Law Society allow them to include a provision in their letters of engagement saying that unless their clients objected at the retainer stage, they would be deemed to have agreed to the firms acting in actual conflict situations. Two years later when the SRA consulted on conflicts as part of principle based regulation they included further relaxations. The body representing the top 100 FTSE companies objected. Nothing daunted, the SRA tried some other relaxations. This

does not apply to the large Scots firms), as has their requirement that all their trainees sign a waiver from the European
Working Time Directive (which the Scots counterparts have
copied). The doctors had the same option and chose not to
go down that path (despite the highly publicised problems
this has caused), believing that the underlying principle was
the right one for their members. Speaking bluntly, if the large
law firms consider that there is commercial value or at least
no commercial downside to retaining the brand and status of
solicitor or Scottish solicitor then the profession may yet survive and thrive.[90] However, there is one last sting in the tail.
The relationship between the legal profession and the public has been a symbiotic one. Each has had need of the other.
Lawyers have always needed clients, but ironically the advent
of ABS and new providers in the market place, means that the
public may no longer need the profession – unless, of course,
it can adapt.

---

time City firms objected – maybe their corporate clients had told them,
enough was enough.
[90] Boon and Levin, *The Ethics and Conduct of Lawyers in England &
Wales*, p. 67 consider that there may even be room for a new concordat
between the profession and the state in recognition of the role of the
large law firms in the economy and on the international stage. This
would depend on the profession's guarantee of ethical behaviour: 'Far
from being redundant, ethics could hold the key to the future of legal
professionalism.'

3

Access to justice: whither legal aid?

Equal justice under law is not merely a caption on the facade of the Supreme Court building, it is perhaps the most inspiring ideal of our society. It is one of the ends for which our entire legal system exists ... it is fundamental that justice should be the same, in substance and availability, without regard to economic status.

Supreme Court Justice Lewis F. Powell, Jr.

In England, justice is open to all – like the Ritz Hotel.

Justice Mathew 1830–1908,
quoted in R. E. Megarry, Miscellany-at-Law (1955)

Access to Justice is a social good: the ability to participate in public redress or resolution systems is a measure of the health of any system of government, particularly in a democracy.

The Law Society of England and Wales,
Access to Justice Review, 2010, para. 1.2

The public good and access to justice

In Chapter 2 I looked at the efforts of lawyers over the years to define the best interests of the public with respect to the profession and professionalism, and how these had come under challenge in recent years. Next I will be looking at how lawyers over the years have sought to define the best interests of the public in relation to access to justice, and poverty legal services in particular, and how here too their efforts to define the public good have come in for challenge. The solution, I will argue, lies in fuller and more comprehensive dialogues between the stakeholders.

'Access to justice' as a phrase can be traced back to the nineteenth century, but as a concept it is a comparative newcomer to the political firmament, coming into frequent usage only in the 1970s. Since then there has been no holding it. Hundreds of books, articles and reports have included it in their title, not to mention a swathe of initiatives from lawyer associations, politicians, governments, charities and NGOs around the world.[1] As the redoubtable Roger Smith noted in 2010,[2] 'In general ... the phrase "access to justice" has a well-accepted, rather vague meaning and denotes something which is clearly – like the rule of law – a good thing and impossible to argue you are against. The strength and weakness of the phrase is in its nebulousness.' In short, access to justice is like 'community' in being a feel-good concept – one that everyone can sign up to with uncritical examination.

Even a cursory examination of the literature reveals that the access to justice debate has many strands. In this century, the principal ones have been about: (a) enhancing state-sanctioned dispute resolution processes; (b) measuring the incidence of justiciable problems and people's response to them; and (c) legal aid and the challenge of providing adequate legal services to those who cannot afford them in a way that is

---

[1] See M. Galanter, 'Access to Justice in a World of Expanding Social Capability', *Fordham Urban Law Journal* 37 (2010), 115; and M. Cappelletti and B. Garth (eds.), *Access to Justice* (Amsterdam: Sitjoff &Noordhoff, 1978).

[2] Roger Smith, 'Justice', *ILAG Newsletter*, March/April 2010.

affordable to the taxpayer and providers. However, new aspects emerge – or old ones in a new guise – almost on a daily basis. Some of the more interesting being: what has geography to do with access;[3] what role is there for public legal education; and could simplification of the law solve significant access to justice problems?[4] The last is a reference to holistic access reform admirably epitomised in the Australian Government's recent *Strategic Framework for Access to Justice in the Federal Civil Justice System*:

> Improving access to justice requires a broad examination of how the system and its various institutions influence each other and work together to support or limit people's capacity to address legal problems and resolve disputes. Reforming one or more of the individual institutions or programs might assist current clients or users but will not provide sustainable access to justice benefits or increase the number or profile of beneficiaries. A whole of system examination is needed.[5]

I agree with this, and would observe that in Scotland the integration of criminal procedure reform and legal aid reform

---

[3] Access: historically seen as geographic and physical, although latterly has come to include affordability also. Scrutinising the distance and difficulty faced by citizens in getting to a provider of poverty legal services with expertise and spare capacity in the area of law relevant to the citizen. In future technology may mean access by phone, web or hologram.

[4] T. Wright *et al.*, 'The Common Law of Contracts: Are Broad Principles Better than Detailed Rules? An Empirical Investigation', *Texas Wesleyan Law Review*, 11 (2005), 399–420.

[5] Australian Government, *A Strategic Framework for Access to Justice in the Federal Civil Justice System: A Guide for Future Action*, 2009, available at: www.ag.gov.au/a2j; www.ag.gov.au/www/agd/rwpattach.nsf.

in the last decade has been a significant step towards a holistic system examination. Nevertheless, for the purposes of this chapter 'access to justice' will be confined to 'access to affordable publicly funded legal assistance', that is, legal aid. In substituting process for outcome – an exchange that only a positivist lawyer would think represents progress – I am, of course, eschewing the temptations of a philosophical discourse on the nature of justice under the law. Nevertheless, just as all roads lead to Rome, whatever strand of the 'access to justice' debate we focus on, we are always drawn back to the appropriate use of state resources. In short, we are in the realm of power and politics. Who gets to call the shots? Who is to define the public good? In the past it has usually been lawyers, but sometimes access to justice is too important to be left just to them. Although praiseworthy in many ways the Gill Review on Civil Justice[6] involved seven judges, six lawyers and two other professionals who were system insiders. Had it been a Royal Commission it is inconceivable that its composition would have been so bereft of laypersons. It is all rather reminiscent of the original legal aid committees set up in England and Scotland in 1950. The Haldane Society suggested that there should be some laypersons on them to represent the public interest. The legal professions successfully lobbied to exclude them. Indeed, over the years it would be fair to say that almost everyone involved with legal aid reform has claimed to act in the best interests of the public and the taxpayer, but somehow we rarely hear the voice of the public itself.

---

[6] Lord Gill, *Scottish Civil Courts Review*, 2009, available at: www. scotcourts.gov.uk/civilcourtsreview/theReport/Vol1Chap1_9.pdf.

The recent consultation by the Ministry of Justice (MoJ) on legal aid reform[7] is reputed to have elicited 5,000 responses, so it may be that some will be from disinterested (but not uninterested) members of the public, but the great bulk are likely to be from organisations with a stake in the process. An opinion poll commissioned by the Legal Action Group (LAG) in November 2010 found that a huge majority of people across all social classes favoured civil legal advice being free for people on average incomes or below,[8] which is certainly not in Kenneth Clarke's (Justice Secretary) Consultation Paper. Indeed, the indications are that the Ministry of Justice intends that the access to justice priorities of the public are to be determined, not from the mass of solid research evidence available to the MoJ, but on a philosophy that rejects early intervention by lawyers and favours the avoidance of courts at almost any cost. This was the very issue against which Hazel Genn remonstrated so powerfully in the Hamlyn lectures only two years ago.[9] So much for evidence-based policy-making.

The history of legal aid

Those who don't know history are destined to repeat it.[10]

[7] See Ministry of Justice, *Proposals for the Reform of Legal Aid in England and Wales*, Consultation Paper CP12/10, Cm 7967 (London: HMSO, November 2010).

[8] Steve Hynes, 'Publicly Funded Legal Advice gets a Ringing Endorsement', *Law Society Gazette*, 11 November 2010.

[9] H. Genn, *Judging Civil Justice*, The Hamlyn Lectures (Cambridge University Press, 2008).

[10] Edmund Burke, adapted by George Santayana, *Reason in Common Sense*, vol. 1 (New York: Dover, 1980).

We stand today on the threshold of what is only the latest, albeit one of the larger, crises to confront publicly funded legal services in its relatively short global existence. However, before we stumble into knee-jerk coping strategies it might be as well to have a brief review of the history of legal aid in the United Kingdom, especially as the recent MoJ Consultation Paper contained a number of historical inaccuracies in the argument for cuts and retrenchment.

For the first few centuries – there is Scots legislation on civil legal aid from 1424 and criminal legal aid in 1587 – although some of the work was paid by the Treasury it was essentially the charitable or *pro bono* model which prevailed. As I argued in Chapter 2, this was a product of the contractualist model of the profession, or noblesse oblige, if you prefer. On the plus side, it did some good and it instilled the values of *pro bono* work in younger members of the profession – rather as law clinics do now. On the downside, it was a severely means-tested, inconsistently applied and variable quality service. Although there are historical similarities between the poor law programmes over the centuries in England and Wales, on the one hand, and Scotland, on the other, the two legal aid systems really came close together with the salaried legal services made available to members of the armed forces during the Second World War to assist them with marital breakdown. It was these that led to the Rushcliffe and Cameron committees, which recommended the introduction of a peace-time legal aid scheme available to a large section of the population. Contrary to Kenneth Clarke's statements as to the aims of the modern legal aid system, Rushcliffe[11] intended legal aid to be available to those on middle incomes as well as the poor, and expected that almost half the civil funding would go to the salaried provision of advice work and divorce. The implementing legislation made provision for this, but the English Law Society, fearful that middle-class privately paying clients would disappear to be the clients of a salaried National Legal Service, persuaded the Lord Chancellor's Department (LCD) to limit the extension of legal aid to people whose income did not exceed £750 a year, and in the 1950s eased the Government away from the notion of a salaried provision on the grounds that it would be too expensive and too difficult to recruit.[12] Moreover, the Labour politicians in Atlee's Cabinet did not see law as a way of enforcing the new welfare rights – and neither had Beveridge, the architect of the welfare state. In short, modern day references to Rushcliffe's vision of legal aid as a central plank in the evolution of the welfare state are somewhat wide of the mark, even though it was a more expansionist provision than Kenneth Clarke would have us believe.

---

[11] Steve Hynes and Jon Robins argue that Rushcliffe intended legal aid to be fourth leg of the welfare state available to all who needed it in *The Justice Gap* (London: Legal Action Group, 2009) p.131.

[12] See T. Goriely, 'Rushcliffe 50 Years On', in A. Paterson and T. Goriely (eds.), *Resourcing Civil Justice* (Oxford University Press, 1996), p. 221. This represented something of a change of heart, possibly reflecting the waning of the collective spirit that had prevailed in wartime, since the salaried components had largely come from the evidence of the Law Society. See M. Zander, *Legal Services for the Community* (London: Temple Smith, 1978), p. 60.

In both countries the civil schemes were the first to be implemented, while criminal legal aid reform took until the early 1960s to be introduced. Despite some hiccups on the way the essential structures which were eventually implemented in Scotland and England and Wales were pretty similar. Over the next twenty-five years the similarities grew. Whatever the wartime position, each evolved into judicare schemes (that is, delivery by the private profession to individual clients) that focused on initial advice and legal representation in the courts (but not tribunals), as the profession demonstrated – not for the last time – an ability to co-opt legal aid reforms. The exclusion of tribunals and defamation, however, was not due to the profession, but originally in part to the personal objections of one influential cabinet minister: Herbert Morrison, who felt tribunals should be simple enough for unrepresented persons and also that defamation cases were ill-advised and should not be encouraged.[13] The next area for reform was advice and assistance, and again the profession resisted the reform for as long as they could before co-opting it. Curiously, the Scots ended up taking the lead not only with advice and assistance reform, but also, some time later, with the legislation taking legal aid out of the hands of the law societies and allocating it to an independent board.

So much for the evolution of legal aid in England, Scotland and Wales until the modern times, when the two systems were pretty much alike: overwhelmingly judicare;

[13] See T. Goriely, 'Civil Legal Aid in England and Wales 1914 to 1961: the Emergence of a Paid Scheme', unpublished Ph.D. thesis, University College, London, 2003, p. 180.

overwhelmingly concentrated in the areas that the profession felt most comfortable in supplying: criminal, family and personal injury; overwhelmingly demand-led; and considerably more expensive in per capita terms than the rest of Europe. How are we to account for this? Space and time do not permit a proper exegesis, but in brief, the principal factors have been a propensity for divorce (which in turn was influenced by being a largely non-Catholic country in the 1950s), a form of welfare state that did not include no fault compensation for accidental injury, a legal system that was too complex and unpredictable to encourage legal expenses insurance, high crime rates and a commitment to the adversarial model of truth-seeking. You will note that I did not include a reference to the European Convention on Human Rights.[14] That is because it has played very little part in the development of the UK legal aid programme.[15] The Convention has played a greater part in other European countries, for example, the expansion of civil legal aid in Ireland or the introduction of criminal legal aid in all of the 'new' entrants to the EU in 2009, but the wide variation in per capita spend on legal aid around Europe indicates that the Convention does not clearly mandate high levels of per capita expenditure in a jurisdiction. Ironically, it may well play

[14] Steven Philippsohn and Trevor Mascarenhas, 'A Class Apart', *European Law*, 87 (2009), 14; *Golder* v. *United Kingdom*, 21 February 1975, cited in Jeremy McBride, 'Access to Justice and Human Rights Treaties', *Civil Justice Quarterly*, 17 (1998), 235–71 at 237.

[15] Its principal impact has been to extend advice by way of representation (ABWOR) before certain tribunals and in defamation cases following the 'MacLibel' case, *Steel and Morris* v. *United Kingdom* [2005] ECHR 103.

a greater part in preserving certain areas of legal aid spend – especially on the criminal side as the cuts planned by the MoJ begin to bite.

The theoretical justification for state-based legal aid

With significant cuts in legal aid the order of the day through-out the United Kingdom, there could be no better time for returning to first principles in re-examining the justification for spending taxpayer's money on publicly funded legal assist-ance. The MoJ Consultation Paper says that the 'Government strongly believes that access to justice is a hallmark of a civil society',[16] but then goes on to indicate that in practical terms only the most needy will be helped – it is as though the NHS were to say we believe in universal healthcare, but only the most needy, those of no or very low income with advanced cancer or a severe heart condition will be helped. Preventive medi-cine will not be practised. So why should the state fund legal aid? In part, because Article 6 of the European Convention on Human Rights mandates aspects of it, if only in fairly modest ways. Yet to say that is merely to beg the question – why is it enshrined in the Convention in the first place? A quote from the iconic liberal Justice Brennan of the US Supreme Court is of assistance here:

> When only the rich can enjoy the law, as a doubtful luxury, and the poor, who need it the most, cannot have it because its expense puts it beyond their reach, the threat to the

[16] Paragraph 1.1.

68

existence of free democracy is not imaginary but very real, because democracy's very life depends upon making the machinery of justice so effective that every citizen shall believe in the benefit of impartiality and fairness.[17]

As the quote implies it is an almost universally accepted tenet of modern political philosophy, as it was for thinkers as diverse as Rousseau, John Stuart Mill and Dicey, that effective and equal access to the law is a fundamental part of the rule of law and thus the democratic legitimacy of the state. Substantive legal rights, the argument runs, are of little value to citizens if the latter lack the awareness, capacity, facilities or wherewithal to recognise, or enforce, these rights or to participate effectively in the justice system. This then is the argument for providing legal services (broadly defined) to those who cannot afford to pay even reasonable and proportionate legal costs.[18] It is sometimes also argued that legal services are good for individuals whether they appreciate it or not, but this argument too often amounts to a brand of paternalism that has few modern-day supporters. No, as Tammy Goriely and I argued fifteen years ago,[19] assisting people to vindicate their legal rights is a societal or a public good every bit as much as it is an individual or private one. It may not directly benefit the user of legal services, but it should 'contribute to a more procedurally

---

[17] Justice Brennan, 1956. See Law Society of England and Wales, *Access to Justice Review* (London: Law Society, 2010), para. 2.2.

[18] See Cappelletti and Garth (eds.), *Access to Justice* and T. Goriely and A. Paterson, 'Resourcing Civil Justice', in Paterson and Goriely (eds.), *Resourcing Civil Justice* (Oxford University Press, 1996), pp. 3–12.

[19] Goriely and Paterson, 'Resourcing Civil Justice'.

just society – that is, a society in which law is helped to meet its intended goals, is applied more fairly, and achieves greater public support'. In the words of John Griffiths, the argument for providing publicly funded legal assistance is:[20]

> Not that they are a form of wealth, not that they are good for people, not that social change will result from distributing them, but rather that the just operation of the legal system demands a more equal distribution of the use of facilities collectively believed to be important to the realisation of legal entitlements and protections.

If procedural justice is the moral imperative for publicly funded legal services – how far should this be taken? What does equality of arms mean? It does not mean that the state is seeking to equalise the respective strengths of the protagonists, or that each is being given a club of equal size. The state is not seeking to alter any advantage between the parties in terms of the substantive merits of their case. The rules of procedure are designed to provide a level playing field and legal aid is part of this. But it is *not* trying to bring about a draw by evening up the teams. It *is* trying to prevent certain forms of unfairness. The interesting question is, what does the state treat as unfair? If one party is emotionally weaker, or less able to cope with the stress of litigation, or has time constraints that the other does not, or if one is economically much stronger than that other – all factors which arose in the thalidomide litigation[21] – the state will generally not

---

[20] 'The Distribution of Legal Services in the Netherlands', *British Journal of Law and Society* 4 (1977), 282.

[21] T. Harvey and C. Munro, *Thalidomide: The Legal Aftermath* (Farnborough: Saxon House, 1976).

see its role as being to eliminate such differences.[22] However, it may try to ameliorate them through legal aid. Should legal aid include the right to a lawyer of your choice? They must be minimally competent, but need they be a top-flight QC? Does it even need to be a lawyer? Would an in-court adviser, a paralegal or even a McKenzie friend comply with the state's minimum obligation? Presumably, part of the answer will depend on whether we retain the adversarial form of truth-seeking[23] even at the small claims level. Equally, the importance of what is at stake will have a bearing on these matters.

Challenges for legal aid and access to justice

So much for the justification for publicly funded legal assistance, but it leaves a range of questions unanswered, which have

---

[22] Equality of arms might be said to require us to restrict the services available to the wealthy, but this would be impractical. Thirty-six years ago Marc Galanter in 'Why the "Haves" come out Ahead', *Law and Society Law Review*, 9 (1974), 95 showed how repeat players have structural advantages in the resort to law, while Bryant Garth in 'Rethinking the Legal Profession's Approach to Collective Self-Improvement: Competence and the Consumer Perspective', *Wisconsin Law Review* (1983) 639, argued that in a market for legal services those with more money will always be able to pay for more of a lawyer's time, and will therefore be better prepared. Any serious attempt to create equality would need to impose rigid restrictions on how repeat players use the courts and on how they are represented. Yet restricting access for the powerful is rarely suggested and almost never implemented. If it were, one suspects that it would soon prove ineffective as the powerful learnt how to circumvent the restrictions.

[23] If one accepts the tenet of appropriate dispute resolution, that certain cases are best dealt with by litigation, then in these cases legal aid should be available to those unable to afford the proportionate costs of a lawyer.

become more prominent in modern and post-modern thinking on legal aid in recent years. These are: the role for strategic planning; questions of affordability, rationing and prioritisation; and the problem of integrating supply and demand.

Strategic planning

As we saw earlier, publicly funded legal assistance was not part of Beveridge's master plan for the welfare state, whatever the alarmist talk of nationalising the legal profession which emerged when the Scots' bill was going through Parliament in 1949 might have suggested.[24] Atlee's Government was looking for a tactical solution to the demand for affordable legal services for those whose marriage had broken up during the war. The legal profession were a little more strategic, seeing legal aid as an opportunity to be paid by the state for what previously they had done with little reward, while gaining control of the early development of legal aid in the United Kingdom. The Rushcliffe Committee did propose legal advice centres staffed by salaried lawyers, which were to be run by the Law Society. However, during the 1950s the profession ensured that this aspect of the legislation was never implemented. This successfully delayed the introduction of a mixed model of legal aid provision in United Kingdom for twenty years, inhibiting the development of a strategic delivery model for legal aid programmes.[25] Both the charitable and the judicare models of

[24] See 1949 SLT (News) 30, 39, 71 (Hansard HC, vol. 465, cols. 2001–2).

[25] Part II of the 1972 Legal Advice and Assistance Act gave the English Law Society power to employ salaried solicitors to give legal assistance, but the Treasury never came up with the funds to implement the provision.

legal aid delivery were individuated, reactive and unfocused in approach – responding to perceived demand rather than pro-active planning. It took the arrival of law centres and a few radical firms in the early 1970s to see the tentative emergence of a strategic, proactive use of legal aid. Although critical comments from the Royal Commissions on legal services eventually prompted the Government to take control of legal aid away from the law societies, they found consistent planning beyond them; indeed, in one particular nine-year period from 1986 to 1995 England had seven different policy initiatives for legal aid.[26] Nevertheless, by the turn of the century, commentators, policymakers and researchers throughout the United Kingdom were all agreed that the way forward for developed legal aid jurisdictions was the complex, planned mixed model, that is, a delivery mechanism that consisted of a strategic blend of the private profession, salaried lawyers and paralegals in the voluntary sector emanating from a focused partnership between suppliers and policymakers.

Affordability, rationing and prioritisation

In the light of the impending legal aid cuts on both sides of the border, I doubt whether I have to make the case for affordability being a key issue for legal aid. However, today's dire economic climate makes it easy to forget that we have not always been so philosophical when it comes to rationing access to justice. Only thirteen years ago Michael Zander wrote in his Hamlyn Lecture, 'The rationing of legal aid is an attack on

---

[26] See Goriely and Paterson, 'Resourcing Civil Justice', p. 30.

access to justice.'[27] As with other aspects of access to justice, much depends on whose perspective and whose definition of the public good is to prevail. Being a demand-led budget the Treasury were always cautious about escalating expenditure, which helps to explain why, when Rushcliffe favoured a universal legal aid package, the Treasury phased in the various elements over the ensuing twenty years. So when Kenneth Clarke says, 'The current scheme bears very little resemblance to the one introduced in 1949'[28] – and should by implication be cut back to 1949 levels – he overlooks the fact that criminal legal aid was not included in the 1949 package as a result of the Treasury's incremental policy. Is Mr Clarke therefore proposing to abolish criminal legal aid? He is not. However, it seems that the Treasury's concerns about the legal aid budget have never been properly allayed. One senses that the spending ministries were allowed to contemplate expansion over the years only because they were prepared to embrace the tactical use of hidden cuts in the civil programme through not uprating allowances and eligibility with inflation.[29]

Part of the ever-present pressure for cost-cutting emanates from the figures that show that over the years the real cost of legal aid not infrequently rose faster than inflation, productivity or GDP (Figure 3.1).[30] What was the explanation for

---

[27] M. Zander, *The State of Justice*, Hamlyn Lectures (London: Sweet & Maxwell, 1999), pp. 10–11.

[28] Ministerial Foreword, Consultation Paper CP12/10, *Proposals for the Reform of Legal Aid in England and Wales*, p. 3.

[29] See Goriely and Paterson, 'Resourcing Civil Justice', pp. 20–2.

[30] See Frank Stephen, *Legal Aid Expenditure in Scotland* (Edinburgh: Law Society, 1999) and Ian Magee, *Review of Legal Aid Delivery and*

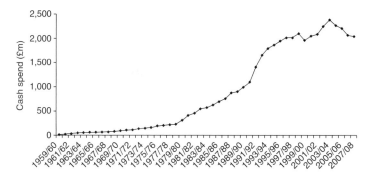

Figure 3.1   English and Welsh expenditure on legal aid (2008 prices, cash)
Source: Legal Aid Board/Legal Services Commission.

this? One theory put forward by economists and much loved by the Treasury was supplier-induced demand; namely, that the profession was manipulating the scheme to its own advantage. The profession, of course, hotly denied such charges – and with justification it turns out. The research into the phenomenon found some evidence for perverse incentives in fee maximisation, but also that the bulk of the cost drivers lay outwith the profession,[31] including: (1) the creation of more and more offences, and the passing of more and more legislation without proper impact assessments;[32] (2) playing intergovernmental

Governance (London: Ministry of Justice, 2010), pp. 26–7, available at: www.justice.gov.uk/publications/docs/legal-aid-delivery.pdf.

[31] Ed Cape and Richard Moorhead, 'Demand Induced Supply? A Report to the Legal Services Commission' (London: Legal Service Commission, 2005) and Richard Moorhead, 'Legal Aid – System Failure or Broken Law?', *New Law Journal*, March (2010), 403.

[32] Law Society of England and Wales, *Access to Justice Review*, paras 2.44–2.49; Cape and Moorhead, 'Demand Induced Supply?'.

budget games – over VAT on legal fees and increasing court fees – both of which involve huge payments to the Treasury, but somehow are never mentioned in debates about what legal aid is costing us; and (3) the failure of government agencies (central and local) to fulfil their legal obligations.[33]

Nonetheless, the evidence of ever-rising expenditure had one effect. Most commentators came to accept that the potential demand for legal services was always going to out-strip the supply available. The optimism of the 1960s and 1970s that access to justice was an aspiration that could be achieved was replaced by a pragmatism that accepted that expenditure would have to be curbed and priorities for expenditure set. In other words, that legal aid would have to be rationed.[34]

Integrating supply and demand

Although, therefore, most commentators have accepted for some time that in a world of limited resources some form of

[33] See Law Society of England and Wales, *Access to Justice Review*, paras 2.32–2.35 and L. Janes, 'What are Legal Aid Lawyers For?', in J. Robins (ed.), *Closing the Justice Gap* (London: Solicitors Journal, 2010) p. 32, available at: www.solicitorsjournal.com/Pictures/Web/k/l/p/Closing%20 the%20Justice%20Gap.pdf.

[34] See Roger Smith: 'No government would allow legal aid spending to rise at the same rate that it did through the 1980s and 1990s ... Access to Justice and legal aid will only escape the axe – and rightly so – if they can be supported by arguments that the government of the day can understand and accept', 'The Justice Gap: Whatever Happened to Legal Aid?', New Law Journal, 159 (2009), 866. Galanter, 'Access to Justice in a World of Expanding Social Capability', has noted, 'In a world ... where claims of injustice proliferate, we cannot avoid the necessity of rationing justice. Justice is not free. It uses up resources.'

rationing for legal aid is required, unfortunately, the access argument that justifies publicly funded legal assistance affords us little guidance as to how best to prioritise such expenditure, while still pursuing the goals of access to justice and equality of arms. Historically, the attempted solutions to that problem have varied depending on who is defining the public good in this area. Economic theory may suggest that demand in the market is the driver for supply modifications, but it is almost axiomatic that the need for legal aid stems from a failure in the market. In truth, for the first forty years of its existence in the United Kingdom the demand for publicly funded legal assistance, or the unmet need for legal services as it is sometimes put, has *de facto* been largely determined by suppliers. And during that time they were overwhelmingly lawyers in private practice. As we saw earlier, they resisted changes that might have undermined their control of the delivery model especially when legal aid was administered by the law societies. At that time, the need, as well as the unmet need, for poverty legal services was defined by what the private profession were prepared to supply and how they were prepared to supply it. Divorce, personal injury and crime the profession understood, but social welfare law (housing, employment, debt and social security) they did not; they neither recognised need in that area – in part because they were not trained in it – nor did they think that practice in that area could be made to pay. When others sought to tap into that market, through the use of advertising, DIY law shops or law centres,[35] the

---

[35] M. Zander, *Lawyers and the Public Interest* (London: Weidenfeld & Nicolson, 1968).

law societies viewed such competing definitions of need with grave suspicion and sought to suppress or confine them, as they had done with the salaried elements in the original legal aid legislation. Indeed, in relation to advertising and law centres it was only when the Government of the day threatened to intervene that the profession gave way. In truth, the unmet legal need identified in the 1960s and 1970s was heavily influenced by supplier-defined notions of need. Whatever the problem was, private lawyers were the answer. Reformers might point to a lack of awareness by the public of legal rights and remedies, but until the Hughes Commission on Legal Services in Scotland[36] it was assumed that the solution lay in identifying private lawyers with the capacity and the competence to provide such remedies in locations and at prices that suited the public. If Hughes recognised that legal services need not be delivered by lawyers, it took until 2000 when Professor Dame Hazel Genn (as she is now) devised the concept of a justiciable problem in order to break away from the teleological element in defining legal problems and supplier-defined conceptions of unmet need.[37] By placing the consumer at the centre of modern needs assessment these studies have begun to transform delivery strategies. The re-discovery that people's responses to justiciable problems turn more

[36] Royal Commission on Legal Services in Scotland, Cmnd 7846 (Edinburgh: HMSO, 1980).
[37] See *Paths to Justice* (Oxford: Hart Publishing, 1999) and *Paths to Justice Scotland* (Oxford: Hart Publishing, 2001) – studies which have now been replicated in twelve countries around the world and repeated several times in England and Scotland.

on the nature of the problem[38] than on party competence or
questions of affordability has provided us with the key to the
prioritisation of publicly funded legal assistance. Further, the
studies have shown that justiciable problems come in clusters
and if left untended will tend to cascade, persuading policymakers of the merits of early intervention and preventative
law. Indeed, this was the explicit logic for the Dutch shifting
legal aid expenditure to the early stages with their *lokets* or
legal counters in modern offices throughout the Netherlands.
For once, delivery mechanisms were being determined by clients' perceptions of need rather than those of the provider.
One of the most unfortunate aspects of the proposals in the
MoJ Consultation Paper on legal aid reform in 2010 was that
although the ministry claim that early intervention is still a
key aspect of their access to justice policy,[39] the early intervention they have in mind is not from lawyers, nor is it holistic
(as in the Netherlands). Yet, ironically, the evidence base for
preventative and holistic intervention in England and Wales
is greater than any other jurisdiction.[40]

---

[38] R. Sandefur, 'The Fulcrum point of Equal Access to Justice', *Loyola of Los Angeles Law Review*, 42 (2009), 949 shows that the response to justiciable problems in the United States and England and Wales varies with class as well as the nature of the problem.

[39] See the appearance of Jonathan Djanogly MP before the House of Commons Justice Committee 16 February 2011, available at: www.parliament.uk.

[40] See, e.g., P. Pleasence, *Causes of Action*, 2nd edn (London: The Stationery Office, 2006).

Legal aid in England and Scotland: two jurisdictions divided by a shared tradition?

So how has the bulk of the United Kingdom responded to these three challenges?[41] As we have seen, up until the late 1990s the systems in England and Wales and in Scotland were pretty similar to each other, but in the past decade or so the two systems have been moving in different directions, despite avowedly pursuing the same goal of a complex, planned mixed model. How and why has this come about?

Strategic planning

The real divide came with the Government decision to transfer responsibility for legal aid in both jurisdictions from the profession to independent legal aid boards. The Legal Aid Board (LAB) visited on the Scots had little stated function other than to safeguard the legal aid fund. The English and Welsh Board, established by the Access to Justice Act 1999, was more generously endowed by its creators. Its responsibility for providing poverty legal services in England and Wales was clear *and* it had a policy role, including the gradual transfer of resources towards the Community Legal Service (as civil legal assistance was now called). Further, they had a leader who was prepared to utilise these powers to the full: Steve Orchard. Under his aegis the Legal Aid Board (LAB) thrived. Yes, eligibility was reduced from 77 per cent

---

[41] Space does not permit the inclusion of an examination of legal aid in Northern Ireland, which is largely based on the English model, because the history of its provision has been distorted by the troubles.

of households to 53 per cent, and there were some minor reductions in coverage for legal help (advice and assistance), but expenditure continued to grow in excess of inflation and productivity and on every front Orchard outmanoeuvred his parent ministry.[42] I believe that the Access to Justice Act 1999 has had a bit of a bad press; it has certainly been asserted – sometimes in Hamlyn Lectures[43] – that it was nothing to do with enhancing access to justice and all about cuts. While it is true that it did indeed lead to a reduction in scope, interestingly it did not lead to a decrease in civil expenditure (Figure 3.2); moreover, it had a very ambitious aim to transfer civil funds to early intervention. In my view, at least in relation to strategic planning and wrestling the definition of need away from suppliers, England took a large stride ahead of Scotland at this stage.

Community Legal Service

As its name implies, this was a strategy to make the focus for the delivery of poverty legal services the local area but delivering it through a partnership of the profession, the advice sector, local government and the Legal Services Commission. As Lord Irvine the then Lord Chancellor noted:

> The CLS is the first attempt ever by any government to deliver legal services in a joined up way. It will provide a framework for comprehensive local networks of good

---

[42] Goriely and Paterson, 'Resourcing Civil Justice', p. 30.

[43] See, e.g., Zander, *The State of Justice* and Genn, *Judging Civil Justice*, p. 12.

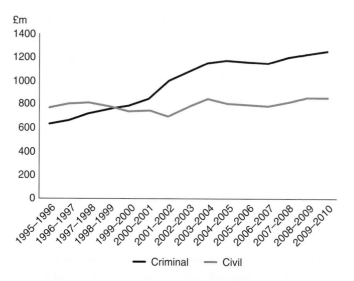

Figure 3.2   Expenditure on legal aid in England and Wales (civil and criminal)
Source: Legal Aid Board/Legal Services Commission.

quality legal and advice services supported by coordinated funding, and based on the needs of local people.[44]

The strategy was very ambitious. Getting the potential partners to come together would involve a huge commitment of staff and resources from the Legal Services Commission, and would work only if there was something in it for everyone. This was the rub, what Orchard was trying to do was to shift resources to Community Legal Services (CLS) and social welfare law and that meant that someone had to give up resources. In principle, re-distributing resources made sense once it was

[44] Quoted by Zander, *The State of Justice*, p. 19.

accepted, as most commentators by then did, that resources for legal aid were finite. The LAB's original work on mapping needs assessment,[45] later replaced by the more defensible Paths studies by Hazel Genn,[46] convinced Orchard that a preventative approach was required, which meant that resources on the civil side had to be front-loaded into advice and assistance, or Legal Help as it was now called. In addition, telephone advice lines and an Internet information service were established. These initiatives have been a success story, but the key part of CLS was the attempt to establish partnerships between local stakeholders and providers charged with (1) assessing local supply, (2) assessing local need and (3) sorting out the mismatches. The first two always made sense,[47] but it was Michael Zander, as so often before, who predicted with uncanny precision exactly why CLS wouldn't work: it was too labour intensive for the Legal Services Commission and local authorities were not prepared to cede power over funding.[48] It was never likely that better resourced areas of the country would be willing to transfer them to poorer areas, or that funders of one form of over-supply would be willing to fund an under-supply controlled by another agency. Eventually, Community Legal

---

[45] Based on proxies for social welfare need, e.g., housing benefit.

[46] Subsequently built on by Pascoe Pleasence and his Legal Services Research Centre team, *Causes of Action.*

[47] Many of the respondents to the recent Review by Sir Ian Magee, *Review of Legal Aid Delivery and Governance*, p. 50 remained of the view that CLS partnerships in local communities were the right way to go.

[48] See also R. Moorhead, *Pioneers in Practice: The Community Legal Service Pioneer Partnership Research Project* (London: Lord Chancellor's Department, 2000).

Services Partnerships (CLSPs) were abandoned by the Legal Services Commission in 2005 and replaced by other, more limited but even more controversial proposals: Community Legal Advice Centres (CLACs) and Community Legal Advice Networks (CLANs). These, too, have run up against the intransigencies and entrenched positions of local organisations.[49] The Legal Services Commission (LSC), as part of New Labour's attack on social exclusion, proposed that CLACs should be one-stop shop centres with multiple services under one roof to tackle the difficulties faced by those with multiple and cluster problems. Once again, the LSC lacked the political clout to force local government to share their vision or funding for local advice by pooling resources with the LSC for holistic advice and assistance provision.[50] Moreover, the political problems of replacing 5,000 traditional firms with up to fifty large-scale providers have proved insurmountable.[51]

The Scots conducted their own Paths research, but continued to be hampered by their unhelpful founding legislation. Although attracted by community legal services,[52] their

[49] See R. Moorhead, *Community Legal Advice Centres and Networks: A Process Evaluation*, (London: Legal Services Research Centre, 2010).

[50] *Legal Advice and the Local Level* (LALL) (London: Ministry of Justice, 1999) found that the five CLACs then in existence were managing adequately, but had been costly and time-consuming to set up. The Magee Review considered that CLACs and CLANs were being rolled out much more slowly than originally envisaged, *Review of Legal Aid Delivery and Governance*, p. 58.

[51] For a critique of CLACs and CLANs and their tendering mechanisms in particular see J. Robins (ed.), *Closing the Justice Gap* (London: Solicitors Journal, 2010), p. 35.

[52] See Scottish Executive, *Review of Legal Information and Advice Provision* (Edinburgh: Scottish Executive, 2001).

principal and rather blunt instrument was Part V projects, since, unlike the position in England and Wales, they could not award social welfare contracts to the third sector as the legislation restricted legal aid money to lawyers. Indeed, some might say that the position was compounded by taking certain social welfare and debt matters out of the scope of advice and assistance without ensuring that there was capacity and funding in the third sector to pick up the slack. However, the Legal Profession and Legal Aid (Scotland) Act 2007 permitted the grant funding of projects with the third sector, and in the last year or two the Scots have begun to get their act together with regard to local delivery assisted by the Home Owner and Debtor Protection (Scotland) Act 2010, which encouraged collaborative service provision at the local level. The Scottish Legal Aid Board (SLAB) has also been given the strategic role under the Legal Services Act 2010 of monitoring the availability and accessibility of publicly funded legal services in Scotland.[53] Thus, at the very time that the LSC has been retrenching to central administration and losing touch at local and regional levels, SLAB has been establishing outposts in other parts of the country – Aberdeen, Ayr, Dundee, Edinburgh, Falkirk, Glasgow, Inverness, Lochgilphead and Orkney – and begun to work closely with the Convention of Scottish Local Authorities and the Government to deliver an integrated advice service.[54]

---

[53] Legal Services (Scotland) Act 2010, s. 141.

[54] To date, at the strategic level, the Scots have been rather more successful in getting stakeholders to work together in relation to CLS than their counterparts in England and Wales.

Policy reform

If Orchard made policy planning respectable for the Commission, his successes in that direction contained the seeds of problems for those who followed him. At some stage the presence of substantial policy teams in both the LSC and the parent ministry was bound to cause trouble, and following the Magee report in 2010 the duplication has been solved by stripping the LSC of its policy team. Part of the reason why Orchard built up his policy team was that for whatever reason the government departments primarily responsible for legal aid in England and Wales – the LCD, then the Department for Constitutional Affairs (DCA) and now the MoJ – have never found it easy to agree a strategy for legal aid in which they had any confidence for more than a year or two.[55] As Crispin Passmore observed in 2010,[56] 'government has been unclear if it wants the LSC to act as controller of the budget, driver of access to justice or regulator of legal aid providers'. Seven major policy initiatives in the nine years from 1986 to 1995 is impressive in anyone's book, but for the wrong reasons. Throughout that time Orchard was the model of consistency, pushing one big idea. Not surprisingly, his policy views were the ones to prevail. Unfortunately, the degree of policy churn in England and Wales has hardly improved in the last fifteen years. In all, nine reports in fifteen years,[57] and thirty consultations since

[55] Hynes and Robins, *The Justice Gap*, p. 29.
[56] 'The Future is Bright', in Robins (ed.), *Closing the Justice Gap* (London: Solicitors Journal, 2010), p. 24.
[57] Lord Mackay's 1995 Green Paper, '*Legal aid Targeting Need*', aid was followed by a White Paper, and when New Labour arrived by another

2006 alone.[58] In the same period the Scots modestly made do with a fraction of these figures. A Consultation Paper in 2000 that wasn't acted on,[59] the Justice 1 Report on Legal Aid in 2001, a Review of Legal Information and Advice in 2004, the Strategic Review on the Delivery of Legal Aid, Advice and Information in 2004 and a further Consultation Paper, *Advice for All*, in 2005 and that's it.

Quality assurance

In Chapter 2 I indicated that quality assurance and re-validation were a coming feature of professional life. One policy reform where the two jurisdictions have been united is over the importance of quality assurance through peer review.[60] The levels of expenditure on legal aid have been such

White Paper in 1998, '*Modernising Justice*', which in turn led to the Access to Justice Act 1999. Stability reigned for a few years until the DCA's Fundamental Review in 2004 – a vehicle for cost-cutting proposals – which was promptly buried. Then we had the Carter Review in 2006, *Legal Aid, A Market-based Approach to Reform*, which heralded CLACs and CLANs, the NAO Report on the procurement of criminal legal aid in 2009, the Jackson Report, *Review of Civil Litigation Costs: Final Report*, in 2010 was closely followed by the Magee Report on legal aid delivery and governance in the same year. The coalition promptly launched a further Consultation Paper CP12/10, *Proposals for the Reform of Legal Aid in England and Wales*.

[58] Consultation Paper CP12/10, *Proposals for the Reform of Legal Aid in England and Wales*, para. 3.24.

[59] See The Scottish Office, *Access to Justice: Beyond the Year 2000* (Edinburgh: Scottish Office, 1998).

[60] A. Sherr and A. Paterson, 'Professional Competence, Peer Review and Quality Assurance in England and Wales and in Scotland', *Alberta Law Review*, 45 (2008), 151.

that policymakers, as in the education and health sectors, wanted the assurance of value for money for the taxpayer. Peer review programmes were introduced in both countries in the early years of the new millennium and are now world leading in their operation. In England the approach has been to audit a sample of civil and criminal firms and providers regionally. By the end of 2010 the Scots had tackled only civil and children's work, but in 2011 the scrutiny was extended to cover criminal work also. Since 2003, the Scots have audited the work of every civil legal aid practitioner in Scotland twice over,[61] and in the period up to 2017 it plans to audit the work of all civil and criminal legal aid practitioners in Scotland on a risk-based approach.

Affordability, rationing and prioritisation

With suppliers and funders each blaming the other for the rises in legal aid expenditure in England and Wales in the run up to the new millennium the scene was set for a confrontation. When New Labour came into power, Steve Orchard found an unexpected ally in Derry Irvine. In opposition he had been coruscating in his criticisms of Lord Mackay of Clashfern's Green Paper,[62] which proposed the prioritisation of expenditure within a fixed budget on legal aid. Yet a few short months later when appointed Lord

---

[61] This is a unique database in its comprehensiveness – and it shows that the overwhelming majority of civil legal aid lawyers deliver good quality legal services to their clients, although effective communication can be a problem.

[62] 'Legal Aid Targeting Need'.

Chancellor, Irvine[63] demonstrated that where legal aid was concerned he was prepared to be every bit as radical as Lord Mackay.[64] Faced with an ever increasing criminal legal aid bill, which looked even more alarming when (1) high cost cases were transferred from the responsibility of the courts and (2) the Human Rights Act was presaged, the LCD civil servants produced a bold plan. This formed the basis of the 1999 Access to Justice Act for England and Wales and the LCD drove it through despite a bruising fight with the Law Society, which saw Irvine resorting to allegations of 'fat cat' legal aid lawyers – the last refuge of a justice ministry in a corner – in retaliation for the Law Society's emotive campaign of 'Justice Denied' posters which soured relations with the Government for a considerable period. Each side used claims as to the public good as political footballs, and Kenneth Clarke's moves to cut expenditure by £350 million in late 2010 were predictably accompanied by similar claims that his proposals were for the public good and references to gravy trains and budgets out of control. What then did the Access to Justice Act do?

Introducing a cap on legal aid expenditure

Establishing a cap on legal aid expenditure put pressure on the civil budget as it lost out to criminal legal aid and human rights

---

[63] Known to posterity, perhaps unfairly, for instructing the use of expensive Puginesque wallpaper in his refurbished official apartments.

[64] One correspondent to *The Times* remarked that it was fortunate that the Lord Chancellor was proposing wide-ranging reforms to legal aid: 'Had he sought to merely paper over the cracks, this would have proved prohibitively expensive.' G. Whiting, *The Times*, 5 March 1998, p. 39.

cases. Lord Irvine indicated that this was indeed the intention of the Access to Justice Act 1999: 'The only money that is left for civil legal aid is what is left over out of the budget after the requirements of criminal legal aid have been met.'[65] Contrary to the publicity accompanying Kenneth Clarke's Consultation Paper, the cap has held expenditure more or less in check for at least a decade (see Figure 3.2). The Scots schemes have remained without a cap, that is, demand-led, but tight administration and efficiency savings have kept spending firmly screwed down, although the recession saw civil legal aid applications rise by 40 per cent in the three years to 2011.[66] On both sides of the border the policymakers sought to check legal aid expenditure – particularly on the criminal front – through the introduction of fixed and standard fees. Although not at first, eventually the reforms had the desired result (Figure 3.3). Indeed, the Magee Review noted that expenditure on English criminal legal aid 'has fallen in real terms by 12 per cent over the past 5 years.'[67] Nor was the position dramatically different in Scotland.[68]

Adjusting scope: the position of money claims

One reason that commentators so often claimed that the Access to Justice Act 1999 was nothing of the sort, is that undoubtedly its most infamous provision was that the LCD decided to take money claims (primarily personal injury cases) out of legal aid. This was intended to free up money not only for crime and for

[65] Hansard HL, vol. 596, col. 918, 26 January 1999.
[66] Press release, SLAB, 18 February 2011.
[67] Magee, *Review of Legal Aid Delivery and Governance*, p. 7.
[68] Civil legal aid expenditure was less in 2010 in real terms than in 2000.

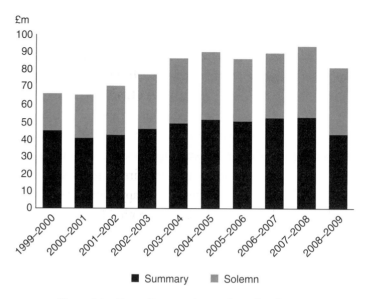

Figure 3.3   Expenditure on Criminal Legal Aid in Scotland
Source: Scottish Legal Aid Board.

human rights, but also for an expansion of legal assistance in social welfare law cases. To make the reduction in scope work they had to encourage claims companies (which they did by subjecting them to light-touch regulation) to boost the use of conditional fees (no fee if you lose and increased fees if you win), and to deal with the risk of losing by fostering 'after the event' (ATE) insurance to pay the other side's expenses if you lost. To reinforce the reform package the statute required losing defenders to pay the conditional fee as well as the winning client's insurance premium. The Scots did not take money claims out of scope – thus, bypassing the whole edifice of conditional fees, ATE insurance and the rampant operation of claims companies so vividly criticised in the 2010 Jackson report[69] and further attacked by Strasbourg in the *Naomi Campbell* case.[70] How should we account for this? There were three reasons. First, the reform was triggered by the insurance companies in London lobbying the LCD to have money claims taken out of scope on the grounds that too many bogus claimants were receiving legal aid in personal injury cases.[71] There is no trace of them lobbying in Edinburgh. Secondly, Whitehall civil servants looked at the same phenomenon as the Scots policymakers, but each drew different conclusions. The LCD saw that approximately 90 per cent of legally aided personal injury cases cost the state nothing once contributions and the recoveries were taken into account. This they took to be an indication that the market could, with a little encouragement take responsibility for money claims without the need for a state subsidy. The Scots with the same data concluded that the fact that around 90 per cent of money claims were being concluded at no long-term cost to the state was an indication of excellent value for money. Thirdly, conditional fees do not work in Scotland as they do in England. There is no equivalent legislation allowing the uplift to be awarded against the losing party as well as the premium for the ATE insurance. The Scots limited experiment with ATE insurance then failed through adverse selection. This was perhaps fortunate, because unlike

---

[69] Lord Jackson, *Review of Civil Litigation Costs: Final Report* (London: Ministry of Justice, 2010), available at: at www.judiciary.gov.uk/ Resources/JCO/Documents/jackson-final-report-140110.pdf.

[70] *MGN Ltd* v. *United Kingdom* 39401/04 [2011] ECHR 66.

[71] This has been a clear case of 'be careful what you wish for', since the insurance companies have ended up on both sides of money claims in the last decade.

England and Wales the use of the uplift in fees had only been subjected to light-touch regulation in Scotland.

Eligibility

This is an area where the policy in England and Wales has rarely risen above the tactical. Whenever the cost per case rose over the years the policymakers responded by not up-rating financial eligibility limits in line with inflation. When legal aid was launched in 1950, 80 per cent of the population was eligible for civil legal aid on income grounds – even more generous than Rushcliffe had proposed (a matter overlooked by Mr Clarke in his call for a return to the 1949 scheme). By 1973, the proportion had fallen to 40 per cent, it was briefly boosted thereafter and by 1998 it was still 52 per cent. However, it had fallen to 41 per cent by 2005, 29 per cent in 2008 and even with the intervention of Lord Bach and the recession it was only around 36 per cent in 2010.[72] Scotland had mirrored these fluctuations pretty faithfully up until the 2000s, but in 2010 in a stunning reversal the Scots, taking advantage of an unexpected dip in criminal legal aid expenditure and having the courage to back their fiscal calculus and judgement, decide to double the upper disposable limit for income and to bring eligibility back up to 75 per cent of the population again. It was not nearly as costly a gesture as it sounds, because sliding-scale contributions meant that the middle-income earners ended up paying for the whole cost of their legal assistance through their contributions. Why

[72] See Hynes and Robins, *The Justice Gap*, pp. 21 and 71 and Law Society of England and Wales, *Access to Justice Review*, para. 2.29.

then would they use legal aid? First, because they could spread contributions over several years, secondly, because legal aid rates for lawyers are considerably cheaper than private rates and, thirdly, because the real advantage of legal aid is that it acts as an insurance policy against the risk of having to pay the other side's legal expenses should the assisted party lose. It does mean, however, that financial eligibility was dramatically different in the two countries at the start of 2011 – and that was before Mr Clarke's proposed cuts in eligibility.

Integrating supply and demand

Here again the Scots and the English have embraced contrasting strategies. Orchard was a strong believer in the value of empirical research into the operation of the justice system and its value for enhancing policy. Discovering that approximately 30 per cent of the profession did 70 per cent of the legal aid work, Orchard concluded that if 70 per cent of the profession was doing only 30 per cent of the work then they were largely dabblers and likely to be doing the work inefficiently. He began to explore avenues for raising the overall quality of work done by legal aid providers and also concentrating supply. Step one was optional contracts or franchising that conferred advantages on quality-assured suppliers. Once that network was in place, he and the LCD/DCA could move on towards the second step, exclusive contracts. The English expected in this way to go from 11,000 providers to 5,000 or so,[73] and that is what has occurred. Mr Clarke intends it to drop still further.

[73] M. Zander, *The State of Justice*, p. 13.

The Scots have, and had, roughly the same 70:30 split as the English. However, with their large tracts of rural and semi-rural communities the Scots preferred to retain low-volume providers to the creation of advice deserts. There was no policy to concentrate supply.[74] Even by 2011 the Scots had neither franchising nor contracting. There was a substantial decline in Scottish provider firms from 1999 to 2009, but these were largely from the 70 per cent who did relatively little legal aid work, and in 2010 there was a significant rise in provider firms in response to the shortage of other work during the recession (Figure 3.4). Ironically, in that ten-year period the top 20 per cent of legal aid firms in Scotland were doing more legal aid at a time when low-volume providers were dropping out, so there was a *de facto* concentration of supply in Scotland, but not as a result of a strong push from policymakers.

The vulnerabilities of contracts

Anyone who was watching the legal aid scene in England towards the end of 2010 was aware of the vulnerabilities of contracts. The fiasco over the tender for family contracts was a body blow to the sector. The number of family contracts was reduced by 46 per cent in the 2010 tendering round, with good firms losing out altogether and new, untried firms getting the cases for which they had bid. The subsequent court challenge was upheld, so everyone was then aggrieved: the old firms, the new firms, who thought they had contracts and had taken

---

[74] Although the peer review quality assurance programme contained a mild pressure towards the concentration of suppliers.

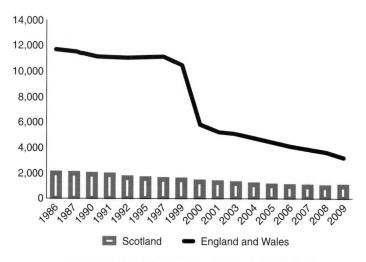

Figure 3.4   Concentration among Civil Legal Aid providers in
Scotland, England and Wales
Source: Legal Services Commission and Scottish Legal Aid Board.

on staff, the LSC and the Government. However, Mr Clarke's
plans to remove much of family legal aid from scope may solve
the contracting problem in another way.

To some economists the ineluctable conclusion to
using contracts to control supply is to introduce competitive
tendering on price – or best value tendering (BVT) as it is now
euphemistically known – however, to those with longer memories the fear is that, as with competitive tendering in the services sector in the early 1990s, it will lead equally ineluctably to
a race to the bottom in quality terms. Indeed, it was in part for
this reason that Avrom Sherr and I began our work on quality
assurance and peer review in the hope that we could develop
a robust and reliable mechanism for establishing a quality

floor before the policymakers got to the stage of implementing competitive tendering.[75] There have been several attempts by the LSC to introduce competitive tendering in England and Wales in recent years – the last attempt foundering because the profession was more effective in the lobbying of politicians than was the LSC. I do not see Kenneth Clarke making that mistake and his Consultation Paper made clear competitive tendering was on its way.[76]

Investing for the future

A rather more praiseworthy effort to influence supply – this time for the future – was the LSC's scheme, established in 2000, to provide grants to legal aid firms to fund the tuition fees for legal practice courses and the salary of trainees. This was an innovative and far-sighted scheme to invest in the next generation of legal aid lawyers, encouraging in particular those who came from disadvantaged backgrounds. Up until 2010 over 750 trainees had benefited in this way. Unfortunately, the MoJ then axed the £2.6 million per annum scheme on cost grounds, claiming that there were now 'too many lawyers chasing too little work', a claim hotly rejected by LAG and others.

The canny, not to say frugal, Scots have had no such scheme, although they did finance research into the question of where the legal aid lawyers of the future were to come from, from which they drew the fortunate conclusion that there were

---

[75] A. Sherr, A. Paterson and R. Moorhead, *Lawyers the Quality Agenda* (London: HMSO, 1994).

[76] See Ministry of Justice, *Proposals for the Reform of Legal Aid in England and Wales.*

enough graduates coming through who were still interested in doing legal aid. It will be interesting to see whether this assessment is correct or whether, once the effects of the recession are behind us, it proves to have been somewhat optimistic.

State salaried legal aid lawyers

Around the world other common law jurisdictions have experimented with the establishment of a salaried defence service as the counterpart to the Crown Prosecution Service. The private Bar has been universally hostile to such initiatives – either for principled concerns over independence or conflict of interest or out of a dislike of unfair competition. The Scots introduced them two years before the English in 1998, but in each country the set-up costs and the problems associated with establishing a clientele ensured that the experiments have been limited ones. England has now relegated them to status of 'Green Goddess' fire engines,[77] but the Scots have expanded the service to seven offices and seventeen salaried lawyers able to offer traineeships to replenish the ranks of criminal legal aid practitioners in the future. In response to a need to make an 8 per cent cut in the legal aid budget for 2011/12 the Scottish Government proposed a substantial expansion in the number of public defender (PDSO) solicitors and offices, in order to take over 60–75 per cent of the duty solicitor weeks in their existing or planned areas of expansion. Following negotiation

---

[77] So-called after the auxiliary fire appliances used in England and Wales in the latter part of the twentieth century as back-up if the main fire fighting services were on strike.

with the Law Society a considerably smaller expansion was agreed with much less of the duty work.[78]

On the civil side, the English LAB and LSC have long supported a range of law centres, as well as funding the salaries of third-sector specialist advisers, but had no salaried solicitor programme of their own. In Scotland, there has been no support programme for law centres as such, although they can provide judicare and employ salaried solicitors funded under the 2007 Act. That Act has, however, allowed SLAB to create a range of projects covering almost the whole of Scotland with salaried solicitors in regional offices, in-court advice schemes and salaried special advisers: a total of twenty-six posts and counting. The beauty of these initiatives is that they allow for targeted provision, giving them a flexibility which judicare lacks.

Overall

So there we have it. In just over a decade the English had embraced a cap on expenditure, a major reduction in scope; there was the debacle of conditional fees and ATE premia and a spate of accompanying litigation; franchising, exclusive contracts, imminent BVT, the concentration of the supply base, a continuing slide in eligibility, the replacement of CLSPs by a handful of CLACs and CLANs, frequent policy shifts, and to cap it all the proposed transfer of the LSC into Executive Agency status within the arms of the MoJ. All of that before

---

[78] The proposed figure was a 15–35 per cent expansion in the duty work in areas where the PDSO already operated.

Kenneth Clarke's cuts had begun. The Scots had, and so far have, avoided each and every one of these and delivered more access to justice, on a non-cash limited basis and at a lesser per capita cost than the rest of the United Kingdom. How can we account for this?

Explanations

Each jurisdiction has been pursuing much the same object-ives – but in different ways. If one was being unfair to the Scots it could be said to have some resemblance to the story of the tortoise and the hare. England wasn't able to maintain the momentum of the pace that Steve Orchard set. The less febrile approach of the Scots has paid far greater dividends in the long run.

The comparative problem

Part of the difference is due to the fact that the problems in the two jurisdictions have not been the same. The Scots simply didn't have the very high cost criminal cases that have proved such a drain on the English budget.[79] This is an ironic silver lining stemming from the fact that as more corporate and financial institution headquarters in Scotland have migrated to London, so too have the fraud trials. Again, the scale of the system in England is massive, creating a supertanker effect.

---

[79] In 2008 1 per cent of Crown Court cases took up almost 50 per cent of the criminal legal aid budget in England and Wales. See the Carter Review, *Legal Aid, A Market-based Approach to Reform* (London: Department for Constitutional Affairs, 2006), p. 27, para. 43.

Size does matter. The Scots budget is a fourteenth of its English counterpart. Moreover, the civil service is much thinner on the ground than in Whitehall. This ensures that some of the policy work on legal aid simply has to be done within SLAB. Further, the Scots have been more successful in altering their criminal procedures – both at the serious and the not so serious (solemn and summary) levels – in recent years in ways that reduce the cost of the justice system, including the burden on legal aid. At the same time, the Scottish courts have largely lost their ability to award legal aid to SLAB, which is making for greater consistency and efficiency gains.

Leadership

As we have seen, significant elements in the Access to Justice Act 1999 were endorsed or inspired by Steve Orchard. His support for concentrating the supply base and for re-directing resources to CLS and for CLSPs went along with a Commission with strategic and policy responsibilities. Despite the reduction in scope, Orchard was respected because he understood the system at the sharp end and what it was trying to do. After his departure his successors, whatever their managerial skills, lacked his knowledge of legal services on the ground and were, unfairly, not always viewed as having his commitment to poverty legal services. Scotland has been fortunate that Orchard's counterpart there, Lindsay Montgomery, has had a sure-footedness that not all Orchard's successors have demonstrated.

In my view, leadership in legal aid terms really matters in two main areas. First, keeping control of the budget and, secondly, managing key stakeholders. Clearly, the two issues are related. Unlike the LSC, SLAB's administrative processes, turn-around times and overall business efficiency have improved at a time when SLAB was able to hold costs down and to convince the Government that they were in control of the budget. Even when the LSC appeared to have kept its spend within the cap, the National Audit Office (NAO) were unconvinced that it was exercising sufficient financial controls, for example, because of alleged over-payments to suppliers of £24.7 million in 2008/09 and £76.5 million in 2010.[80] In a similar vein, the Magee Review asserted that the LSC had no effective budget forecasting.[81] The Government is, of course, the key stakeholder to manage. Orchard was a past master at this, and his constancy in policy terms, and his general self-confidence in his understanding of the system, meant that the Government trusted his judgement. His successors, charged with running a non-departmental public body that actively shaped supply in its market rather than reactively paying for what the existing market supplied, as it had done in the past, found it harder to command the Government's confidence, while in contrast the Scottish Government had confidence in SLAB's Board and its chairman and CEO in particular.

What of the profession? Steve Orchard commanded the respect of the profession even when they didn't agree

[80] National Audit Office, *Report of the Comptroller and Auditor General to the Houses of Parliament on the Community Legal Service Fund and the Criminal Defence Service accounts for the year ended 31 March 2010* (London: The Stationery Office, 2010). For a critique of the NAO Report see LAG, 'Accounting for Overpayments', *Legal Action*, January 2011, 3.

[81] Magee, *Review of Legal Aid Delivery and Governance*, p. 30,

with what he was doing. His successors were not so fortunate. Repeated clashes with them over the contracts and later the re-negotiation of the contractual terms in a downwards fashion, all provoked the profession. Contracting had led law firms to bulk up to do more legal aid work, which meant that when the LSC tightened the terms of the contracts, although the firms threatened to strike, they found that they had made themselves too dependent on LSC funding to cease doing legal aid work. This only embittered them. Nor did it help that the LSC was not seen as supportive by the profession. Thus, a NAO survey of solicitors found that 36 per cent of respondents perceived the LSC as 'unhelpful' and 29 per cent believed the LSC did not fully understand the system.[82] Hillary Sommerlad's work shows constant complaints by legal aid practitioners about bureaucracy from the LSC. As the Law Society reported to Sir Ian Magee, they wanted 'less micro-management by the LSC'[83] and many providers complained that the LSC were 'still bureaucratic, slow and unduly burdensome'.[84] The constant change in legal aid policy didn't help either. The MoJ was no better than the LSC on this score, but LSC were the ones that providers dealt with on a day-to-day basis. SLAB did have skirmishes with sectors of the profession, but the relationship between SLAB and the profession was better than in England, as evidenced by the latest solicitor survey conducted by SLAB,[85] which found high levels of satisfaction with the

---

[82] Quoted in Magee, *Review of Legal Aid Delivery and Governance*, p. 30.

[83] Magee, *Review of Legal Aid Delivery and Governance*, p. 58.

[84] Magee, *Review of Legal Aid Delivery and Governance*, p. 75.

[85] Solicitor Survey 2010, available on SLAB website at: www.slab.org.uk.

board's processes – particularly its on-line application system, which is the envy of the rest of the United Kingdom and is now attracting interest from abroad.

Finally, the LSC failed to engage effectively with the public. They even dropped the iconic legal aid brand in place of several new brands with little public recognition. The Scots, on the other hand, retained the logo and conducted positive research on brand recognition. Indeed, the success of the logo spawned a range of imitations.

The way forward: the complex, planned mixed model

Both jurisdictions have been striving to introduce a complex, planned mixed model of publicly funded legal assistance. Whether we can continue to pursue this vision will depend on the depth of the cuts and the intransigence of the Treasury. It will also depend on the frequency of unexpected interventions, such as the *Cadder* case[86] on the need for police station legal advice, and rises in VAT. Both jurisdictions will continue to confront the three challenges of strategic planning, rationing and integrating supply with need.

As for *strategy* the oversight role for access to justice contained in both Legal Services Acts will mean that SLAB and the LSC's successor body will come increasingly to see their role as shaping the market to deliver legal services for the public good.[87] You would not expect me to forecast the demise

---

[86] *Cadder v. Her Majesty's Advocate* [2010] UKSC 43.
[87] See Magee, *Review of Legal Aid Delivery and Governance.* p. 57.

of evidence-based policy-making and neither will I. The argument for robust empirical research from independent academics as well as the vigorous in-house teams has never been stronger. However, there are concerning signs that Mr Clarke's reform proposals in 2011 have turned their backs on preventative assistance from legal services providers and the lessons that have been learned from the needs assessment studies. It is not clear that most stakeholders would consider this to be in the public interest, nor will we see a diminution in the drive for better quality assurance. The taxpayer's and the Treasury's insistence on value for money is not a passing fancy. We will, of course, see jurisdictions seeking to make do with proxies for quality assurance such as accreditation, on the grounds of cost, or striving for the holy grail of outcome assessment[88] so prevalent in other fields – medicine, higher education and teaching – which will continue to elude the researchers' best efforts in the legal realm. However, as I indicated in Chapter 2, the pressure for the re-validation of practitioners – for long the policy for airline pilots and now policy for UK doctors – has already been mooted by the Thomson Review in Scotland and the Legal Services Consumer Panel of the LSB in England and will not pass legal aid lawyers by just because they are subject to peer review. Rather, I suspect that the pressure will grow, as it is in the Netherlands, for all private lawyers to be peer reviewed, as legal aid and many corporate lawyers now are, and this will include pleaders before courts and tribunals.

---

[88] See Passmore, 'The Future is Bright', in Robins (ed.), *Closing the Justice Gap*, p. 25.

As for *affordability and rationing* the severity of the impending cuts will doubtless re-ignite the flames of a debate that has raised its head on several occasions in the last few years: should we be separating the civil and criminal budgets? Irvine's quote in 1999 and Kenneth Clarke's Consultation Paper are not re-assuring for those who have been fearful for some time that one unintended consequence of the Human Rights Act will be to prioritise the criminal spend over the civil spend[89] as it is in so many other countries. England and Wales, until relatively recently, have been unusual in having even an approximate balance between the civil and the criminal budgets.[90] Some commentators,[91] therefore, have pushed for separate ring-fenced budgets for civil and criminal legal aid, but Magee came out against splitting funds[92] and it is difficult to see how a split budget would have dissuaded Kenneth Clarke from turning on civil legal aid. Interestingly, it is not thought that the English profession favours ring-fencing nor does the MoJ or SLAB. One budget retains flexibility, which is what led to the expansion of salaried lawyers in Scotland as well as the dramatic raising of the upper eligibility limit last year.

---

[89] Hazel Genn in *Judging Civil Justice* highlighted the threat to the civil spend from an ever expanding criminal spend. As Genn noted, national targets in England and Wales were for less use of civil courts and more use of criminal courts; similarly, in Scotland the national objectives are largely criminal and there are very few overtly civil justice ones.

[90] In the Netherlands, civil legal aid expenditure, very unusually, outstrips criminal legal aid expenditure.

[91] See Hynes and Robins, *The Justice Gap*, at pp. 111, 132 and 135. But see Robins (ed.), *Closing the Justice Gap*, p. 67.

[92] Except perhaps for social welfare law, 'I conclude that there is no compelling argument for separation', p. 4, Executive summary.

New money

Perhaps less surprising is that at a time of impending cuts there is plenty discussion of the need for new money; but interestingly the realism on rationing legal aid that has largely prevailed in the last decade has entailed that almost no one expects it to come from the taxpayer. However, the preferences for where it should come from tend to reflect whose preferences we are talking about. Thus, the Treasury, the spending ministries and the professionals want the *client* to pay more. This could come in a number of guises:

(1) A *statutory claw-back* applied, as in the case of repayment of student loans, once an assisted party reaches a certain salary level.

(2) A *flat contribution* towards defence costs.[93]

(3) *Conditional fees and contingency fees.*[94] The Law Society in England and Wales considers that conditional fees do not give rise to conflicts of interest or access problems (in fact, they give rise to both).[95] Multi-party cases are ineligible for legal aid and are rarely supported by conditional fees. It is very unlikely that cases of borderline or moderate merit will be run by lawyers on conditional fees, nor will those requiring large amounts of scientific or technical expert evidence.[96] This is what made Kenneth Clarke's

---

[93] See H. Bellingham, 'Worth Fighting For', in Robins (ed.), *Closing the Justice Gap*, p. 14.

[94] See Law Society of England and Wales, *Access to Justice Review*, paras. 4.9–4.14 and Jackson, *Review of Civil Litigation Costs*, pp. 125–33.

[95] Law Society, *Access to Justice Review*, para. 4.30.

[96] P. Todd, 'Declining Popularity', in Robins (ed.), *Closing the Justice Gap*, p. 59.

proposal to exclude clinical negligence cases from legal aid so troubling. Contingent fees might help, but unless damages are increased those most severely injured will suffer the most, as money needed for their care has to go to pay their lawyer.

(4) *Contingent legal aid fund or supplementary legal aid fund.*[97] The first of these schemes originated in Hong Kong to cover personal injury cases. The applicant pays a fairly low fixed percentage of any winnings into the legal aid pot. It has worked well in Hong Kong, but it is only of value in a narrow range of cases. Mr Clarke's Paper recommends it for any clinical negligence cases that receive exceptional legal aid funding in the future. So if the exclusion from scope doesn't get you the SLAS will. However, the professional bodies are split over the value of such a scheme. Its introduction is favoured by the English and Scots Bars,[98] and opposed by the English Law Society because it would be a threat to conditional fees.

(5) *Legal expenses insurance.*[99] For many years policymakers have longed to boost the take up of legal expenses insurance (LEI) in the United Kingdom to the levels seen in Germany or Sweden, but do not know how to achieve

---

[97] Jackson, *Review of Civil Litigation Costs*, pp. 134–41.

[98] Robins (ed.), *Closing the Justice Gap*, p. 14.

[99] N. Kinsella, 'Evolution Not Revolution', in Robins (ed.), *Closing the Justice Gap*, p. 43 and Hynes and Robins, *The Justice Gap*, p. 70. See also M. Kilian, 'Legal Expenses Insurances: Preconditions, Pitfalls and Challenges', unpublished conference paper, Research into Practice: Legal Services Delivery in a New Decade, LSRC Legal Aid Conference, Cambridge, 2010. See also Jackson, *Review of Civil Litigation Costs*, pp. 71–93.

it. There has never been much support for it being made compulsory. To boost LEI would require a cultural shift supported by education, regulation and financial incentives, for example, tax breaks. Moreover, as Richard Moorhead has recently observed,[100] 'most commentary on legal expenses insurance agrees that until our legal system is cheaper and more predictable, legal expenses insurance is unlikely to work'. Even the threat of major cuts to scope is unlikely to change things, since those most likely to take out LEI would be those contemplating using it, thus producing adverse selection. This is why LEI typically excludes divorce and crime. As we know, the former area is just where the bulk of the English cuts in scope in 2011 are aimed.[101]

Equally unsurprisingly, consumer groups and commentators have suggested that the new money should come from the profession – a proposal that has provoked a predictable reaction from the profession. The options put forward include:

(1) *Pro bono* This, of course, is simply a reversion to the original charitable model of legal aid that prevailed for centuries in the United Kingdom, and, as I argued in Chapter 2, is part of the contractual model of professionalism. However, in the last decade and more it has seen a resurgence in England and Wales.[102] In Scotland, the Faculty

---

[100] Moorhead, 'Legal Aid – System Failure or Broken Law?'.

[101] Law Society of England and Wales, *Access to Justice Review*, paras 4.5–8 and 4.33–4.36.

[102] Of particular note is s. 194 of the Legal Services Act 2007.

of Advocates has launched two *pro bono* initiatives in the last twenty years, and the solicitors' branch and particularly the Government legal service have begun to show real interest since 2008. *Pro bono* isn't strictly speaking new money – its new resources – however, in parts of the United States there are mandatory *pro bono* schemes in terms of which those who opt not to send their associates to small claims courts can make a donation to pay for someone else to do the *pro bono* work on their behalf. This is new money. There remains, however, an uneasy tension between *pro bono* and legal aid – is a commitment to the former simply an excuse for the Government to cut back on the latter?[103]

(2) A *levy* on the profession as a variant on mandatory *pro bono*.[104]

(3) A *10 per cent reduction* of existing legal aid fees, which many lawyers consider to be inadequate in any case.[105]

(4) *Interest from lawyer's client accounts.* This is one that the MoJ seems quite keen on judging by the Consultation

---

[103] G. Bindman, 'What Money could Buy', in J. Robins (ed.), *Pro Bono: Good Enough?* (London: Solicitors Journal, 2010), p. 11, available at: www.solicitorsjournal.com/pictures/web/s/h/d/SJ%20Pro%20Bono.pdf.

[104] Passmore, 'The Future is Bright', in Robins (ed.), *Closing the Justice Gap*, p. 29. There are approximately 150,000 regulated lawyers in the United Kingdom in 10,000 firms and chambers. A levy of £100 per lawyer would raise £15 million – a structured levy based on turnover etc. averaging £5,000 a firm would produce an additional £50–£60 million. Alternatively a levy of 1 per cent of profits would produce £35 million.

[105] Ministry of Justice, *Proposals for the Reform of Legal Aid in England and Wales*, ch. 7.

Paper,[106] having got wind of the French CARPA scheme. Most law firms hold client's money and earn interest thereon. As we saw in Chapter 2, under the law of agency these funds belong to the client (unless there is an agreement to the contrary). Even after the House of Lords reminded the profession in the 1960s of this proposition,[107] the solution found left the law firms retaining the smaller interest amounts. When aggregated these could still produce tens of thousands of pounds for law firms when times are good. Seeing that in the rest of the common law world this money is used to fund law libraries, legal education and legal aid, the MoJ has decided that legal aid is the most deserving of these causes and in future the aggregated interest should go to legal aid.[108] The professional bodies, not surprisingly, are fiercely hostile to this proposal. In my view there are two arguments against the proposal. First, that as the American experience tells us, the fluctuations in interest rates make the use of this as a source of legal aid monies very unsatisfactory from a planning perspective. Secondly, the argument for not returning all the interest to clients (less bank charges) was that it would be prohibitively expensive to do so. In these days of computers that argument really no longer holds good. The more radical

---

[106] Ministry of Justice, *Proposals for the Reform of Legal Aid in England and Wales*, ch. 9.

[107] *Brown* v. *Inland Revenue* 1964 SC (HL) 180.

[108] A Law Society Committee recommended this in 1994, but the proposal was defeated by the large law firms. G. Bindman, 'No Substitute', in Robins (ed.), *Closing the Justice Gap* (2010), p. 21.

proposal, therefore, is to say no to the Ministry and return the money to the clients.

(5) The *polluter pays* principle.[109] Possible targets include the financial services sector who outsource some of their costs to the courts and generate huge debt advice issues; central and local government who are often responsible for poor decisions that require those affected to challenge them for not getting their decisions right first time. In the same vein, the English Law Society has recently been championing a tax on alcohol sales to fund legal aid, because drink plays a major part in many forms of criminal behaviour.[110]

(6) Rather differently, there has also been talk of bringing in new *third party funders*[111] (ABS, hedge funds, client credit facilities,[112] insurance companies and claims companies), but it must be doubted if the first two will really be much attracted by legal aid clients.[113]

---

[109] See Moorhead, 'System Failure or Broken Law?'. See also the Law Society of England and Wales, Response to the Legal Aid Reform Consultation Paper, *Green Paper Proposals For the Reform of Legal Aid in England and Wales* (London: Law Society, February 2011), available at: www.justice. gov.uk/consultations/legal-aid-reform-151110.htm.

[110] R. Rothwell, 'Increase Alcohol Tax to Fund Legal Aid, says Law Society', *Law Society Gazette*, 15 November 2010.

[111] See Law Society of England and Wales, *Access to Justice Review*, para. 4.15.

[112] 'Tougher Legal Funding over next 5 years', *Scottish Legal News*, 24 November 2010.

[113] See Peter Cashman, 'Third Party Funding: A Changing Landscape', *Civil Justice Quarterly*, 27:3 (2008), 312–41 and Jackson, *Review of Civil Litigation Costs*, pp. 117–24.

Expenditure control and prioritisation

If there isn't enough new money – surely a safe bet – what other options are there? The traditional routes, as we have seen, are to cut costs through eroding eligibility, increasing contributions, reducing fees and paring back scope still further. Kenneth Clarke proposes to use all of these. As for prioritisation, England and Wales are already part way down this route by virtue of the Access to Justice 1999 Act with its exclusion of money-generating claims. Kenneth Clarke is proposing to sweep away much of family legal aid, except domestic violence, child abuse and child abduction. Instead, he will fund mediation. Unfortunately, mediation depends for some of its efficacy on the fact that if it fails the parties can resort to the court. So removing the ability to go to court is likely to undermine mediation. Criminal legal aid, however, is to remain largely sacrosanct, because of the Human Rights Act. Lord Irvine's quote in 1999 and Kenneth Clarke's Consultation Paper strongly suggest that one unintended consequence of the Human Rights Act will be to prioritise the criminal spend over the civil spend. In reaction to this, we will be fortunate if we escape the spectacle of civil lawyers arguing that criminal lawyers should take a bigger share of the cuts and vice versa. Indeed, there is a real risk that the Treasury will seek to play the game of divide-and-rule among the stakeholders. Already the Law Society of England and Wales has been suggesting that a significant element of the savings needed in the south could come from reducing payments to the Criminal Bar. It is scarcely surprising that in both England and Scotland there have been suggestions that the legal aid authorities should share in the misery.

Integrating supply and demand

Careful reading of the Consultation Paper and the appearance of the Justice Minister before the Justice Committee of the House of Commons[114] in February 2011 suggest that although the MoJ is still committed to early intervention, this commitment is only where someone else is paying for it and its not coming from lawyers. Any commitment to a holistic approach to advice cannot survive such a philosophy. Preventative,[115] targeted action aimed at multiple and clustering problems should feature strongly in the complex, planned mixed model of the future, as will public legal education. This is the route travelled by the Dutch with their *lokets*, and the LSC did at one stage try to follow them by introducing a free initial two hours of advice, but the politicians were not willing to support it. Many people think that some kind of triage function to get individuals to the right agency or source of help first time is what is required, and I am hopeful that this will be looked at carefully in the post-Gill initiatives. The very successful Highland project has many of these features. Clients with legal problems are referred from Citizens Advice Bureaux from all over the Highland region and Orkney to the Inverness office, which has six salaried lawyers employed by SLAB. The cases are assessed and offered to twenty-eight legal aid firms around the region. If they do not wish to take them up, the salaried lawyers will do them. This is effective partnership working and is a model

[114] Djanogly, before the House of Commons Justice Committee, 16 February 2011.
[115] See Richard Susskind, *The End of Lawyers?* (Oxford University Press, 2008), p. 231.

we could roll out elsewhere. However, not the least depressing aspect of Mr Clarke's proposed cuts in employment, welfare, debt and housing advice in England and Wales is its seeming rejection of the needs assessment work and preventative intervention to avoid the cascade effect. Without such intervention, it is difficult to see what the value of public legal education to enhance party competence will be.

New providers

The lessons from needs assessment studies will also have implications for the supply side. In a complex, planned mixed model, the mix of providers will include:

(1) The *private profession*, although there are concerns as to where the next generation will come from.[116]
(2) *Salaried lawyers* employed in law centres or by SLAB/ LSC as public defenders (PDSO) or in the Civil Legal Assistance Office.[117]
(3) *Paralegals* employed by SLAB or in the third sector doing advice work including as in-court advisers.[118]

---

[116] Catherine Baksi, 'Where Will the Legal Aid Lawyers of the Future Come From?', *Law Society Gazette*, 28 October 2010.

[117] In Scotland there are only just over thirty salaried lawyers employed by SLAB for civil and criminal work. Here there is much to be learned from the experience of community law clinics in Ontario and New South Wales. Roger Smith, 'Special Delivery', in Robins (ed.), *Closing the Justice Gap*, p. 16 and Michael Mansfield, 'A Fresh Vision', in Robins (ed.), *Closing the Justice Gap*, p. 8.

[118] This encourages local decision-making with a transparent and nationally co-ordinated network of service providers. Lay representation is part of the Home Ownership and Debtor Protection Act strategy in Scotland.

(4) *Student law clinics*: these are prevalent in English and Welsh law schools, and following the outstanding work done by my colleague Professor Donald Nicholson in establishing the award-winning student law clinic at Strathclyde University, more are being established in Scotland. I believe that student clinics have a real part to play in the complex, planned mixed model because they embody a partnership with the profession, opportunities for corporate social responsibility and *pro bono*, significant development opportunities for students and recruits for legal aid lawyering in the future.

(5) *ABS*, for example, Co-op legal services.

New forms of delivery

The mix in the complex, planned mixed model of the future will also involve new ways of delivery. As Richard Susskind observes,[119] we need to move from the working practices of the cottage industry to the business efficiency world of alternative sourcing, better project management, improved workflow systems and shared service arrangements. Otherwise the debate will simply be about new ways of funding old-fashioned legal services providers. If we are to pay more than lip service to the Treasury's mantra – more for less – new forms of delivery are a necessity.

(1) *Self-representation and McKenzie friends*: although aware that these are the likely result of the proposed cuts in

[119] Susskind, *The End of Lawyers?* (paperback edn, 2010).

England and Wales in 2011, the MoJ is maintaining that more self-representing parties will not greatly add to the length or cost of cases. The experts consider that this is an unlikely reading of the research data on the issue.[120] There would be much to be said for looking at the experience in California, where very significant sums of money have been invested in the last decade to support litigants who are unable to afford legal representation.[121]

(2) *Outsourcing and unbundling*: Richard Susskind suggests[122] that costs can be reduced through the standardisation of routine and repetitive work and the computerisation of services, through the use of call centres, and through video-conferencing and decomposing. The last is the splitting up of the discrete tasks in legal work and allocating each to the least expensive sources – provided quality is not sacrificed to cost. It was first advocated by Forrest Mostyn in the United States for low income clients in the guise of 'unbundling', but now the same techniques are being used by City law firms in outsourcing work to India and elsewhere.

(3) *Telephone advice lines*: this was one of the real successes of the English Legal Services Commission. Free legal advice lines can meet public education needs, triage needs and

---

[120] Lawyer Watch, 'Litigants in Person: What the Research Really Says', posted on 16 December 2010 by Richard Moorhead, available at: http://lawyerwatch.wordpress.com/2010/12/16.

[121] Bonnie Hough, 'Access to Justice by Investing in Courts', unpublished paper, International Legal Aid Group conference, Wellington, New Zealand, 3 April 2009, available at: www.ilagnet.org/papers.php.

[122] Susskind, *The End of Lawyers?* (2010 edn).

advice needs. Telephone advice helps to overcome geographic barriers and advice deserts, and is available when the public needs it in the evenings and weekends, not just during working hours. Over time this will be integrated with web advice and interactive holograms. While research tells us that some people like face-to-face advice, others positively prefer the phone. It is very cost effective: only £30 million out of the £2.1 billion currently spent on legal aid in England and Wales goes on telephone advice. On average telephone sessions cost half of face-to-face advice and the satisfaction rate is 90 per cent compared with 70 per cent for face-to-face. By driving down the cost base of delivery it has been suggested that we can help twice as many people for the same money or the same number at half the cost.[123] However, the success of phone advice should not lead it to be seen as a panacea. It follows that the proposal in the 2010 Consultation Paper on Legal Aid Reform that in future the sole gateway to publicly funded civil legal help should be through an advice hotline[124] is one that should be viewed with caution. Maybe the arrival of desktop-to-desktop high-definition video across the Internet will provide a further breakthrough.

(4) *New technologies:*[125] high quality legal advice can be delivered by new business models based on expertise in retail

---

[123] LAG, 'Accounting for Overpayments', p. 138; J. Trigg, 'Citizen Power', in Robins (ed.), *Closing the Justice Gap*, p. 51.

[124] See Ministry of Justice, *Proposals for the Reform of Legal Aid in England and Wales*.

[125] See Susskind, *The End of Lawyers?*.

services. Better information and advice will put clients in control, since technology can help to build party capability through empowerment. 'This is a step beyond current notions of public legal education that, rather than trying to make clients more like lawyers by teaching them their rights and responsibilities, this is changing the legal and advice world to meet clients as they are'.[126] Already there are a range of web entry points – DirectGov, Community Legal Advice, Legal Aid Direct and Citizens Advice Direct – which can assist in a variety of ways from awareness raising to the use of standardised documentation. On-line triage will assist in determining if the public need an expensive lawyer or if a cheap advice system will do. They can also help with the referral task – not simply an Egon Ronay guide to service providers listing their performance details, reputation, peer review results, IPS record, but who is available and at what cost.[127] Such tools would replace the old directories of the past and be of assistance to other practitioners as well as voluntary agencies. Technology will also help with automated forms and document assembly for wills and letters. Susskind argues that we can expect to see the continuing provision of no-cost legal information systems that are easily accessible and digestible: Bailii, the Statute Law database,

---

[126] Passmore, 'The Future is Bright', in Robins (ed.), *Closing the Justice Gap*, p. 26.

[127] As Susskind notes, reputational systems can help to avoid people selecting poor quality lawyers based on price: *The End of Lawyers?*, pp. 108–13.

a Wikipedia of UK law, video clips, legal information systems for the layman. Alas, he may be too optimistic, while such systems may currently be free, they cost money and in the long run someone has to fund them.

Conclusion

Access to justice is vital to a functioning democracy and the rule of law. However, legal aid exists in a world of infinite demand and all too finite resources. What matters then is the just or proportionate use of resources. This places it squarely in the realm of politics. If, as Steven Lukes asserts, politics is about who is able to have their definition of the situation accepted by the rest of the world,[128] then the last twenty years has witnessed a seismic power shift in the United Kingdom. In the past the profession largely defined the legal needs of the public and how they would be met, but in recent years this has become a more contested terrain where other stakeholders (policymakers, the Treasury, taxpayers, clients and politicians) have contributed to the definition of legal need and the public good, and the recognition that the providers of publicly funded legal assistance need not be lawyers. True, there is a risk that the depth of the proposed cuts emanating from the Treasury will mean that it is they that will define the public good with respect to access to justice in the foreseeable future. I have said enough, I hope, to indicate that I do not consider that such a scenario could be considered progress. If access

[128] S. Lukes, *Power: A Radical View*, 2nd edn (Basingstoke: Palgrave Macmillan, 2005).

to justice is too important to be left to the paternalism of the private profession, it is equally true that it is too important to be left to the rivalries of the legal aid authorities and local government or to the tender mercies of the Treasury. In truth, no one stakeholder in the field has a monopoly of wisdom. To the neo-contractualist the real challenge for policymakers and providers is how to work together with funders and other stakeholders. Whether you look on it as 'Big Society' thinking or a war-time coalition the prize is the same: a partnership in which all are committed to the best use of the scarce resources available. The example of the Law Society of Scotland's Quality Assurance Committee, where the profession, SLAB and the public work successfully to quality assure legal aid providers, is but one illustration that this can be done.

It will not, however, be easy – the demise of the Legal Services Commission tells us that. To make partnership thinking work requires all sides to eschew the temptations of political point-scoring and sniping from the sidelines. Here I believe that Scotland's recent track record is considerably better than that in England and Wales. Spending ministers in England and Wales seem to find it difficult to refrain from labelling legal aid lawyers as 'fat-cats' or asserting that the United Kingdom has a compensation culture, when the research,[129] and Lord Young's own Report,[130] does not support this.[131] How

---

[129] James Hand, 'The Compensation Culture', *Journal of Law and Society*, 37 (2010), 569.

[130] Lord Young, *Common Sense, Common Safety* (London: Cabinet Office, October 2010).

[131] Lord Neuberger, 'Swindlers (including the Master of the Rolls?) Not Wanted: Bentham and Justice Reform', Bentham Lecture, UCL Laws

refreshing also if commentators were to cease re-cycling the half-truth that the United Kingdom has the highest spending legal aid programmes per capita in Europe. The Government's own research told them that when one looks at the total spend on the courts (including prosecution costs *and* legal aid) the United Kingdom is not out of line with its northern European counterparts.[132] If Scottish policymakers can resist such temptations – and they have – it would be nice to think that the MoJ could also. Moreover, it is long since time that we got beyond the simple verities of supplier-induced demand. While fee systems do incentivise behaviour among lawyers, the biggest cause of rises in criminal legal aid expenditure in the last decade was the creation of 3,000 new offences under New Labour with the consequent increased risk of imprisonment.

The profession will be called on to play its part. The tensions between the English profession and the LSC over the last decade were not helpful to either party. The lack of trust that developed on both sides led the profession to lobby actively against the LSC and to seek (successfully) to derail their policies (for example, BVT) by negotiating with politicians without the knowledge or participation of the LSC. However, the temptation to reject any reductions in expenditure is both understandable and, I fear, unsustainable, and I applaud the Law Society of Scotland for recognising this. Scottish providers of publicly funded legal services are to be

Bentham Association Dinner, March 2011, available at: www.ucl.ac.uk/laws/alumni/presidents/docs/neuberger_11.pdf.
[132] The European Commission for the Efficiency of Justice, *Fourth Evaluation Report on European Judicial Systems* (Strasbourg: Council of Europe, 2010).

commended for recognising that the crisis in public sector funding means that savings will be required and that tough choices have to be made, especially if Scotland is to retain its demand-led scheme. Suggestions for efficiency gains from new ways of working and the new technologies so close to Richard Susskind's heart must surely be the order of the day. On the other hand, an active debate as to what might constitute a reasonable cost base for legal aid lawyers is long overdue. In other words, setting fee rates that are appropriate for the taxpayer and for the profession remains a major challenge. In a similar vein, we need not only a fair system for fee setting, but also one that handles the auditing of lawyers' accounts appropriately.

Others will rightly expect the legal aid authorities to bear their share of the pain in the shape of efficiency gains, but here too some realism is required. In the world of legal aid boards, Scotland has been exceedingly fortunate in SLAB. It has saved the taxpayer many millions through its increased efficiency, as well as serving the profession and the public better. Declaring an interest and speaking entirely personally, I can see no merit in forcing it into a marriage with a completely different agency such as the Scottish Legal Complaints Commission and even less merit in splitting it into three agencies on the mistaken belief that this will save taxpayers VAT.[133]

Clients, on the other hand, will also have to accept some unpalatable truths about the legal aid system. Assisted

[133] These are but some of the proposals to emerge from the Access to Justice Committee of the Law Society in 2010/2011, although they are not thought to have the support of a majority of the Council of the Law Society.

parties will undoubtedly have to accept greater contributions either directly or through the claw-back mechanism when they recover property in a litigation. Similarly, there may be scope for a Supplementary Legal Aid Scheme, but clients will have to support it through a share of their winnings. Compulsory LEI may be necessary in certain types of case. Moreover, whatever the terms of Article 6(3)(c) of the ECHR, assisted parties are likely to face further incursions on their ability to instruct the lawyer of their choice. For example, that their choices must be rational and proportionate. Why should the state pay for a leading silk to defend an assisted party in a drunk driving case?

In sum, the public interest in access to justice can best be achieved by a partnership between all the stakeholders. In contrast to what is happening in England and Wales – and frankly any solicitor in Scotland who feels that lawyers are being hard done should look at what is happening in other jurisdictions, particularly in England and Wales – legal aid in Scotland, so far, is surviving the recession in reasonable shape. That is largely down to a willingness by the main stakeholders to work together in partnership, as they have been doing in the last few months. The moral is clear. Legal aid is no longer something for the profession or the Treasury to decide what gets delivered where, when and by whom. Now it's down to all of us. We need a coalition of the willing. There is a future for civil and criminal legal aid, but we will have to be nimble of foot.

4

Judges and the public good: reflections on the last Law Lords

In Chapters 2 and 3 I looked at two institutions that are important for a properly functioning democracy: a vibrant legal profession and viable forms of access to justice. With respect to
the former, I suggested that the future of the profession no
longer lies entirely in their hands, but in the ongoing dialogue
between the profession and the wider community. Similarly,
in Chapter 3 I argued that the future of publicly funded legal
assistance was no longer a matter for the profession and the
Treasury, but best approached through dialogues with all the
stakeholders. In this chapter a third institution which is vital
for democracy – the judiciary, and the appellate judiciary
in particular – will be scrutinised. My starting point here is
one that was also identified by Hazel Genn in her acclaimed
Hamlyn Lectures, *Judging Civil Justice*, in 2008: namely, that
in the last forty years we have witnessed a significant growth
in the power of the judiciary vis-à-vis the Executive and the
legislature.[1] This new form of constitutionalism,[2] can be seen
in the expansion of legal remedies, the exponential growth
of judicial review of administrative or government decisions,

[1] Hazel Genn, *Judging Civil Justice*, The Hamlyn Lectures, 60th Series
(Cambridge University Press, 2010), p. 148.
[2] Dubbed by some scholars as 'juristocracy', see Genn, *Judging Civil Justice*,
p. 148.

the evolution of judicial case management, the judiciary's increased role in the running of the courts, the sovereignty implications of devolution, the incorporation of the European Convention on Human Rights into UK domestic law and the establishment of the UK Supreme Court.

All of this has greatly expanded the ability of the judiciary to make determinations of the public interest. Indeed, to paraphrase A. A. Milne, 'declaring the public interest is what judges do best'. They do it in judgments, they do it when performing an administrative role and latterly they have done it as part of what I call an intra-governmental dialogue. For most of the time the judiciary are happy making these decisions as to where the public good lies, because as public servants they feel that they are not only *well* qualified but often *the best* qualified to do this. Where they are deciding cases and the legal test turns on what the public interest is, their assumption seems uncontentious. However, much more often the judiciary are determining what they consider to be the public good in an indirect fashion through their decisions in policy areas or in judicial review cases, or in interpreting the Human Rights Act. In these areas the judiciary's prerogative to determine the public interest does not always go unchallenged, whether by the media, when judges are extending the law on privacy; by Home Secretaries, when their powers are being curtailed by judicial decisions; and by the public, when the Supreme Court fails to protect them from what they see as unfair bank charges. My own bugbear is legal professional privilege: the right of the client to have his or her consultations with his or her legal adviser kept confidential. Over the years this has been raised from the status of a balancing principle against the court's right to the

126

best evidence in the pursuit of truth, to its current status of a 'fundamental human right' as Lord Hoffmann dubbed it in the *Morgan Grenfell*[3] case, which trumps every other competing value, including the protection of life and the vindication of the innocent. Given that Parliament has said on several occasions that there *are* values more important than legal professional privilege, like Bentham I wonder whether in this area the judiciary really have got the public interest right.

Be that as it may, increasingly in recent years the judiciary's views on where the public interest lies with respect to the legal system have emerged from their involvement in the administration of justice. It is here that I anticipate that their authority to determine the public interest is likely to come under the most challenge. Let me give you two examples. As we saw in Chapter 3, in 2009 Scotland's equivalent to the Woolf Report on fundamental reforms to the civil courts in Scotland was produced by Lord Gill, assisted by six other judges, six lawyers and two other professionals who were system insiders. It was strongly asserted when the report was launched that the public interest was at the heart of the Review. Given the composition of the Review team and the very limited nature of the research into public needs and perceptions which they were able to conduct, this assertion must have struck the informed layperson as somewhat curious. Inadvertently, the impression had been given that the public interest in the civil courts was a matter entirely for court insiders.

[3]   *R (Morgan Grenfell & Co.)* v. *Special Commissioners of Income Tax* [2002] UKHL 21.

The second example concerns the use of McKenzie friends as lay advisers or supporters for litigants who are representing themselves in court. In England and Wales we are likely to see more party litigants and lay supporters as legal aid cuts are brought in. Where the supporter is seeking payment for his or her services or to have the opportunity to address the tribunal, it is understandable that the judiciary should be concerned to lay down conditions in relation to such McKenzie friends in the public interest. However, where the issue is simply whether such supporters should be allowed to assist party litigants without pay or rights of audience (a practice which has existed in the United Kingdom intermittently for many years) it is less clear that the public interest can best be determined by lawyers and judges alone without some form of public consultation.[4]

I hope that the point I am seeking to make is clear. Courts are not just for the judiciary and lawyers – they are part of the constitutional fabric of the country. Social contract theory requires that the public interest in relation to the courts and judges is something that everyone is entitled to participate in, the more so where the courts are functioning as the third arm of the state.

---

[4] In Scotland rules regulating *the use* of McKenzie friends or lay supporters have recently been produced by the Rules Councils (comprised of lawyers and judges) without public consultation, even though the topic was widely discussed in the media and before the Petitions Committee of the Parliament. While the Gill Review consulted on the general issue of McKenzie friends, the detailed conditions regulating their use and whether they should have to pay a fee for acting, could not emerge until after Gill.

The dialogue with the Government: inter-governmental relations

While the judicial dialogue with the public has yet to take off,[5] their dialogue with the Executive over the public good has sometimes been too exciting. Usually, but not always, the initiative has come from the Government. The use by governments of senior judges, such as Lords Wilberforce, Hutton, Saville and Cullen, to chair contentious public inquiries is a stratagem that is surely past its sell-by date. One senses a growing wariness from the judiciary over such poisoned chalices, which threaten to exhaust the stock of judicial capital.[6]

Most commonly the dialogue with the Executive comes in cases where the Government is being challenged before the courts, for example, Lord Atkin's dissent in *Liversidge* v. *Anderson*,[7] or the terrorism cases such as *Belmarsh*[8] or *AF*[9] are among the most obvious, but as Adam Tomkins has shown, in many ways it is the High Court foot soldiers who have been

---

[5] In fairness it should be noted that the UK Supreme Court has made strenuous efforts since its establishment to engage with the public through, e.g., the videoing of hearings, leaflets and press summaries of judgments.

[6] Lord Pannick QC is one of a number of voices calling for an end to this practice. See 'The High Price to be Paid if Judges Examine our Historical Events', *The Times*, 17 June 2010.

[7] [1941] UKHL 1, 3 November 1941.

[8] *A & Others* v. *Secretary of State for the Home Department* [2004] UKHL 56, 16 December 2004.

[9] *Secretary of State for the Home Department* v. *AF & Another* [2009] UKHL 28, 10 June 2009.

the unsung heroes of recent security challenges.[10] Of equal scholarly interest, however, are the exchanges that take place outside the courtroom. Occasionally, we will have high profile spats by Home Secretaries complaining about unelected judges thwarting the will of Parliament,[11] or senior judges comparing the activities of the UK Government as reminiscent of the excesses of Nazi Germany.[12] Even more intriguing are the conversations, or attempted conversations, which we don't hear about. The celebrated concordat between Lord Woolf and Lord Falconer followed months of discussions between them and their officials over the new constitutional settlement, including the means whereby the judges would share in the running of the courts and the new judicial appointments commission. Less well known is the fact that there were Scottish concordat discussions between four senior judges and officials in the Scots Justice Department some time later. Unlike the English concordat, neither the fact that the discussions were going on nor the content of the final agreement were published. There can be no objection to the judiciary pursuing

---

[10] 'National security and the role of the court: a changed landscape?', *Law Quarterly Review*, 126 (2010), 543–67.

[11] For example, Michael Howard and David Blunkett. See generally, R. B. Stevens, 'Reform in Haste and Repent at Leisure', *Legal Studies* 24 (2004), 1 at 26. David Cameron and Theresa May made similar critical remarks of Supreme Court decisions on the right to vote for prisoners and sex offenders having the right of review in relation to the Sex Offenders Register in early 2011. See 16 February 2011, Hansard HC Deb., 955, 959 and 969.

[12] See, e.g., when Lords Elwyn-Jones and Lane attacked Lord Mackay's Green papers on the reform of the profession. R. B. Stevens, 'Reform in Haste and Repent at Leisure', p. 15.

their understanding of the public interest in this way, but it was, I think, unguarded politics on the Scottish Executive's part not to publish the outcome of the discussions as occurred in England, for undoubtedly the judiciary in these contexts is involved in politics in Dr Johnson's broad sense of 'relating to government', though not in party politics.

As for attempted conversations, I have in mind when Charles Clarke as Home Secretary asked to meet with Lord Bingham,[13] the senior Law Lord, doubtless in the hope of gaining a steer as to what kind of legislation on terrorists might be acceptable to the House. Bingham, understandably, declined the meeting, since anything he said would be held against him when there was a subsequent challenge to the legislation. The rejection, however, was not understood by the Home Secretary, to whom a suggestion of an intra-governmental meeting made considerable sense. He should have known his history. There have been cautionary tales aplenty when governments have sought to engage with senior judges. I have no doubt Chief Justice Vinson of the US Supreme Court rather regretted that he had not followed Lord Bingham's example when asked by his friend President Harry Truman as to the legitimacy of occupying the Bethlehem Steel Mills, which were about to go on strike during the Korean War. Vinson endorsed the move only to find himself on the end of a 6:3 defeat from his colleagues in the Supreme Court when the inevitable challenge came.[14]

---

[13] See Lord Phillips, 'Introductory Tribute: Lord Bingham of Cornhill', in M. Andenas and D. Fairgrieve (eds.), *Tom Bingham and the Transformation of the Law* (Oxford University Press, 2009), p. xlix.

[14] *Youngstown Sheet & Tube Co. v. Sawyer*, 343 US 579 (1952).

Again, Eisenhower's not too subtle attempt at a dinner to influence Chief Justice Earl Warren in the seminal case of *Brown* v. *Board of Education*[15] by telling him that the Southerners 'are not bad people. All they are concerned about is to see that their sweet little girls are not required to sit in school alongside some big overgrown Negroes'[16] still has the capacity to shock. More recently, the Belgian Government came to grief over its efforts to influence the judges in the appeal court who were determining the legality of the Government's 'bail out' of Fortis, Belgium's largest financial services company, during the global banking crisis by getting an official to talk on several occasions to the husband of one of the judges in the case.[17] The discovery of this led to the resignation of the Justice Minister, reminding us that some conversations should not take place.

On the other hand, one cannot blame Charles Clarke for trying; from a utilitarian perspective he thought it made perfect sense. After all, it was Bentham who scathingly compared the judicial method of making the law as akin to how we train dogs. You wait for them to misbehave and then whack them, and so on until eventually the dog learns the parameters of acceptable conduct. Understandably, successive Home Secretaries would have preferred to avoid the repeated whackings. Moreover, no less a body than the House of Commons Constitutional Affairs Committee has suggested that there is scope for a constructive intra-governmental dialogue between Parliament and the UK's most senior judiciary on broad

[15] 347 US 483(1954).
[16] See Lord Bingham, *The Rule of Law* (London: Allen Lane, 2010), p. 95.
[17] www.timesonline.co.uk/tol/news/world/europe/article5371351.ece.

questions of constitutional and human rights law.[18] Such a dialogue could not extend to individual cases and yet drawing the
line between discussions of principle and issues which might
become justiciable is not easy. This was exemplified when the
Government wrote to Lord Steyn asking that he recuse himself
from the *Belmarsh* appeal, the first really big terrorism case to
come to the Lords. Ostensibly, this was because he had given
an extra-judicial lecture some months before, which they
thought was open to the interpretation that he had expressed
an opinion against the Government's position in the *Belmarsh*
case.[19] Lord Bingham, who opposed the Law Lords speaking in
the House of Lords in debates on matters that they might subsequently be asked to rule on judicially, accepted Lord Steyn's
reluctant conclusion that he should recuse himself. However,
the Government's approach in this matter was at odds with
Clarke's attempt to obtain extra-judicial guidance from Lord
Bingham. Whether it set the ideal tone for the *Belmarsh* case
must be a moot point. The Government lost by 8:1. I shall
return to the case at the end of this chapter. The moral of these
stories, however, is that while intra-governmental dialogues
are desirable to foster the public good, care should be taken to
make them transparent and to avoid too direct discussion of
matters which may become justiciable.

---

[18] House of Commons Constitutional Affairs Committee, HC, 48-I,
2003–4, paras 86, 87. Vernon Bogdanor has also endorsed judicial
dialogues with Parliament as a form of explanatory accountability. See
The New British Constitution (Oxford: Hart Publishing, 2009), pp. 85–6.

[19] 'Guantanamo Bay: The Legal Black Hole' 27th FA Mann Lecture, 25
November 2003.

Separation of powers

I began the chapter with the proposition that judicial power vis-à-vis the Executive and the legislature has considerably increased in the last forty years. Of course, much of this, though not all, has come from conscious decisions on the part of politicians. This has included the transfer of topics from their 'too hot to handle' in-tray to that of the judiciary. Hazel Genn calls this a shifting of reputational risk.[20] However, a significant part of the enhanced power of the judiciary has come from the move from the balance of powers to a separation of powers in our evolving constitution. For centuries the unwritten constitution of the United Kingdom worked on the basis of a balance of powers between Executive, Parliament and the judiciary, with each involved in administrative, legislative and decision-making tasks. However, in recent years, in a process accelerated by New Labour, we have seen the constitution evolving towards a purer separation of powers between these three branches of government. New Labour's manifesto flirtation with a judicial appointments commission was followed by the notorious attempted abolition of the Lord Chancellor on a napkin, the establishment of a UK Supreme Court separate from the Houses of Parliament, the enshrining of the European Convention on Human Rights in our domestic law and the greater role of the judiciary in the running of the courts. This, as Dr Johnson might have observed and Robert Stevens certainly did observe,[21] moved the judiciary more clearly into the

---

[20] Genn, *Judging Civil Justice*, p. 151.
[21] Stevens, 'Reform in Haste and Repent at Leisure'.

political realm, if by politics you understand 'relating to government'. It is curious how little concern this has raised in the circles of academia and the intelligentsia. At a time when we are celebrating the first anniversary of the UK Supreme Court and mourning the passing of Lord Bingham, the greatest judge of his generation, it is easy to forget that our judiciary was not always as well regarded in liberal circles as it now is.

Connor Gearty in his 2005 Hamlyn Lecture, *Can Human Rights Survive?*, explains the disillusionment he felt when the flood of 'dreadful, coercive' public law decisions – his words not mine – emerged from the English courts of the 1980s and early 1990s. How could we expect the judiciary to defend freedom and human rights in the new constitutional settlement if this was the best they could do? Nor was this new, he concluded, because 'there never had been a golden age of judicial good behaviour: this was just a liberal myth'.[22] In reaching this conclusion he was echoing John Griffiths, also of the London School of Economics. Both of them were sceptical of entrusting the defence of human rights to the judiciary.[23] 'The false promise of certainty offered by a supra-political reading of human rights by judges is a short-term fix, producing in

[22] Connor Gearty, *Can Human Rights Survive?*, The Hamlyn Lectures, 57th Series (Cambridge University Press, 2006), p. 3.

[23] 'The trouble with the higher-order law is that it must be given substance, be interpreted, be applied. It claims superiority over democratically elected institutions; it prefers philosopher-kings to human politicians; it puts faith in judges whom I would trust no more than I trust princes. And it will not even make the trains run on time. If we are to create a more just society, we must do it the hard way – without Moses.' J. A. G. Griffith, 'The Brave New World of Sir John Laws', *Modern Law Review*, 63 (2000), 159, 165.

its wake both a legalisation of politics and a politicisation of law. Both are damaging to our democratic culture.'[24] As Gearty went on, it is impossible to squeeze politics entirely out of a system of entrenched human rights law, pointing to the political debates over the composition of the judiciary that have arisen in most countries that have entrusted judges with the definition and protection of human-rights-based truth on their behalf.[25] Gearty was uncomfortable at the prospect of democratically elected representatives passing legislation on what they consider to be in the best interest of the public, only to find their efforts thwarted by a bench of unelected and unaccountable judges.[26] However, despite all this he considered the UK Human Rights Act to have escaped these traps because Parliamentary sovereignty is retained, the judges cannot strike down legislation, but merely make declarations of incompatibility, because the Act is not constitutionally entrenched and Parliament has the power of derogation from the European Convention in situations of public emergency.[27] For the Scots,

[24] Gearty, *Can Human Rights Survive?*, p. 80.

[25] Gearty, *Can Human Rights Survive?*, pp. 87–8. He also notes that judges begin to ape politicians and provides as an example the House of Lords sitting with larger panels – preferring the wisdom of the crown to legal logic. In fact, the larger numbers seem to stem as much from a recognition by the justices that in a panel of five, which justices you get makes a difference. Given that 10 per cent of House of Lords cases split 3:2 the justices have a point. But they are half way to saying that judicial ideology matters.

[26] Gearty, *Can Human Rights Survive?*, p. 92.

[27] Bogdanor, however, considers that the Human Rights Act only achieved a compromise between parliamentary sovereignty and the rule of law which might become unsustainable without restraint on the part of the judiciary and Parliament. See *The New British Constitution*, p. 69.

however, the position is that the courts can strike down statutes of the Scottish Parliament that they deem to be in breach of the European Convention on Human Rights or because they are thought to have transgressed into a reserved area.[28] Further, since Gearty wrote a number of Law Lords have spoken openly of the possibility that under the new constitutional arrangements parliamentary sovereignty is no longer what it once was. Even leaving aside the recent concerns of the Prime Minister and Home Secretary over prisoners' voting rights, it may be that Gearty's concerns were too easily answered.

The challenge of accountability

My argument is that the movement towards a purer separation of powers in the United Kingdom has created an accountability problem, which was not so clamant in the times of a balance of powers. The argument runs as follows: the increased power of the judiciary, the taking over of the courts, the judges' heightened role in judicial appointment, expanded judicial review and the incorporation of the ECHR into our domestic law makes clear, if there was any doubt, that the judiciary are a branch of government in the modern state. As the Lord President indicated on the day[29] he took over running the courts in Scotland, 'If you are part of the community that regards itself as the third arm of government ... you have to recognise that you may have to speak out on matters of importance ... it also provides for putting in written representations

[28] Scotland Act 1998, s. 29(2).
[29] Interview with the Lord President, The Scotsman, 5 April 2010.

on matters of importance to the community'. 'We are public servants, just as parliamentarians are … [We] are providing a public service, but defending [our] independence is part of [our] service to the public.' I agree with the Lord President, but I would go further. As part of government in a democracy the judiciary have not only to be independent, they also have to be accountable. This is the true conundrum behind the question: 'Who guards the guardians?' For it is not simply who is to guard them, but how is it possible to guard them in the first place, because every measure designed to preserve the judiciary's independence simultaneously makes them less accountable to the community they were appointed to serve. That is what some have described as the democratic deficit that confronts us.[30]

In my experience, the UK judiciary in general, and the Law Lords in particular, are divided on their answer to the accountability conundrum:

(1) Some simply see it as a mismatch. Judicial independence is far more important than any issue of accountability. As against this, Robert Stevens has argued that over the centuries the UK judiciary has frequently resisted change they disliked on the grounds of judicial independence – a concept which, as Stevens has observed, does not always lend itself to clear thinking.[31]

---

[30] Stevens, 'Reform in Haste and Repent at Leisure', p. 28.

[31] R. B. Stevens, 'Unpacking the Judges', *Current Legal Problems*, 1 (1993), 2. Stevens shows how the nineteenth-century judiciary ensured that while every other institution was being reformed by the industrious Victorians – 'the franchise, local government, the church, universities, the civil service, the army and navy and even the court structure' – the

(2) One or two regard the issue as resolved in the constitutional settlement of 1688, a view that seems difficult to reconcile with the concept of an evolving constitution.[32]

(3) More frequently the answer is that the increased power for the judiciary comes from Parliament in the first place and they can take it back. Given that there was a strong judicial lobby in favour of the judiciary taking over the running of the courts and that the substantial expansion in judicial review has been judge-led, this cannot be a complete answer. Moreover, for those who think that Parliament cannot now abolish judicial review or reject the incorporation of fundamental human rights into our law, another answer is needed.

(4) A few favour what we may call the Barak answer, after Aharon Barak a former President of the Supreme Court of Israel. As he has argued, someone has to protect the fundamental rights of the minority in a democracy and independent judges are the best solution.[33] One Law Lord told me: 'Obviously the greater the discretion that the judges have the more you can say "why should these people be permitted to take policy decisions which nobody can challenge", but what's the answer, somebody's got to take these decisions.'

---

judiciary alone escaped by relying on the mystique of judicial independence.

[32] That said, there remains a vigorous debate in the United States as to originalism and the Constitution.

[33] Aharon Barak, *The Judge in a Democracy* (Princeton University Press, 2006).

(5) One answer with as much support as any, was to point to existing accountability measures. These include the requirement to give coherent reasons for judicial decisions, mechanisms for appeal, the limits which judges recognise to judicial law-making and what should be left to Parliament, and the commitment to openness and transparency in courts to which I will shortly return.

(6) The final answer was to assert that there is a problem, and that positive steps are needed to be taken to enhance the accountability of the judiciary, especially at the higher levels.

So far, I have eschewed the thorny issue of definition. What is meant by 'accountability' in this context? Like access to justice or judicial independence it is clearly 'a good thing' but difficult to define with precision, since there is no clear consensus as to its meaning. Those who venture into these relatively uncharted waters have tended to distinguish between individual and institutional accountability, but this gets us only so far since, as with the issue of complaints and discipline in relation to judges, there are both individual and institutional elements. Vernon Bogdanor has argued[34] that while politicians can have sacrificial or answerability accountability the same cannot be true for judges. The latter can be held to account only in an explanatory way because of the need for judicial independence. I wonder if he goes far enough. As I shall argue, the dialogues that lie at the heart of appellate judicial decision-making (including the symbolic one with Parliament) are indeed part of accountability. However, Andrew Le Sueur's further

---

[34] *The New British Constitution*, p. 85.

distinctions[35] between probity, process, content and perform-ance accountability for judges are an excellent starting point for getting to grips with this thorny issue. Space does not per-mit me to do full justice to the topic,[36] so I shall confine myself to a discussion of three additional accountability measures which contain both explanatory and answerability elements: (1) addressing the diversity deficit in our judiciary; (2) a re-look at judicial appointment mechanisms, including in the final court; and (3) greater disclosure and transparency.

More diversity

If I may be controversial for a minute, I am a little puzzled that we in the United Kingdom find this so difficult a topic. In Europe it is generally taken for granted that their judi-ciary should be a diverse one. Indeed, at the lower court level in many jurisdictions over half the judges are women. The gender distribution is considerably worse at the level of the higher courts, but they have no doubt as to the desirability of the goal. I see no reason why it should be different here. It is, of course, necessary to be clear what we mean when we say that the judiciary should reflect the communities which they serve. It does not mean that the judiciary should represent society in some crude, identikit way. Even if 5 per cent of

---

[35] See 'Developing mechanisms for judicial accountability in the UK', *Legal Studies*, 24 (2004), 73.

[36] One of the most helpful and sustained attempts to grapple with judicial accountability is Guy Canivet, Max Andenas and Duncan Fairgrieve (eds.), *Independence, Accountability and the Judiciary* (London: BIICL, 2006).

the population have been in prison or votes for the BNP we should not expect 5 per cent of the judiciary to have the same traits. It *does* mean that the judiciary should not be restricted to the white, male middle-class cadre that it very largely was until fifteen years ago.

What are the principal arguments that have been put forward for a diverse judiciary in the United Kingdom?[37]

(1) That it undermines the democratic legitimacy of the judiciary if it is drawn from only one sector of the community.

(2) It is discriminatory to appoint only white males.

(3) It is a waste of a huge range of talent.

(4) It would provide role models to bring a wider diversity into the recruitment pool.

(5) It would increase public confidence in the judiciary and the justice system, particularly among under-represented sectors.

(6) More contentiously, it has been argued that diversity can improve the quality of decision-making in certain areas, for example, in immigration or sexual assault cases.[38] On balance, like Lady Hale[39] I think there may be merit in this argument.

---

[37] See A. Paterson, 'The Scottish Judicial Appointments Board: New Wine in Old Bottles', in P. Russell and K. Malleson (eds.), *Appointing Judges in an Age of Judicial Power* (University of Toronto Press, 2006), ch. 1 and the *Report of the Advisory Panel on Judicial Diversity* (London: Ministry of Justice, 2010).

[38] A measure of empirical support for this position can be found in J. Peresie, 'Female Judges Matter', *Yale Law Journal*, 114 (2005), 1759.

[39] 'Equality and the Judiciary: Why Should we Want More Women Judges?', *Public Law*, (2001), 489.

So where does the controversy come from? Most people in the United Kingdom are not opposed to a diverse judiciary, it is how we bring it about that causes the problem. Many believe that in time the problem will solve itself.[40] Unfortunately, the empirical evidence does not suggest that the trickle-up theory is working. The elevation of female judges into the higher ranks of the UK judiciary has been fairly slow as we can see from Table 4.1. Rather more concerning are two other sets of statistics. Figure 4.1 shows that despite the fact that the gender balance of those with practising certificates in private practice has been steadily moving towards parity in England and Wales in the last twenty years, the proportion of female partners in English law firms has been declining over the same period. Table 4.2 on the face of it seems more encouraging, since it shows that over the last nine years or so 25 per cent of applicants and appointees for shreival[41] posts in Scotland have been female. However, over the same period the proportion of the eligible pool of practitioners who were female had risen to 39 per cent, indicating that the constancy of the 25 per cent figure was not a sign of progress.

Politicians of all party backgrounds have accepted that increasing diversity in the House of Commons will not come about by public exhortations to selection committees. To many

---

[40] The Lord Chancellor in his appearance before the House of Lords Constitutional Committee in January 2011 asserted his belief in the desirability of a diverse judiciary and a belief that it would arrive in due course. The Lord Chief Justice when appearing before the Committee in December 2010 was similarly supportive of judicial diversity, but less sanguine that things would be different in twenty years' time.

[41] In Scotland the sheriff is a judge with powers and jurisdiction somewhere between an English circuit judge and a high court judge.

Table 4.1 *Senior judiciary in England and Scotland by gender*

	2000 Female members of judiciary	2000 Female members as a % of total	2010 Female members of judiciary	2010 Female members as a % of total
Supreme Court/ House of Lords	0	0	1	8
Court of Appeal	2	5	4	11
High Court	9	9	16	15
Court of Session	2	6	5	14
Scottish Sheriff Courts	23	16	29	21

Source: Judiciary websites of England and Scotland.

judges, however, taking diversity into account in the selection process would entail watering down the principle of merit selection. In reality, however, the concept of merit is not an objective one, it is culturally defined. If it were not we would still be largely appointing relatives of the Lord Chancellor, or politicians or politically experienced individuals to judicial posts. Notions of 'merit' as Kate Malleson has shown,[42] reflect the eligible pool of candidates rather than the other way round. Any discussion of 'merit' necessarily begs questions about the kind of judges we want. Apparently neutral qualities (for example, 'authority', 'detachment'), can connote a restrictive background and continue to exclude already marginalised people. There is

[42] K. Malleson, 'Rethinking the Merit Principle in Judicial Selection', *Journal of Law and Society*, 33 (2006), 126–40.

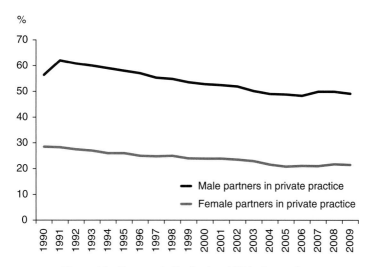

Figure 4.1   Partners in England and Wales by gender
Source: Law Society of England and Wales.

Table 4.2 *Scottish shreival contests 2002–2009*

Scottish Sheriffs and Diversity

Post	Year	Applicants % female	Appointed % female	Aged 41–50 % female
Part-time	2002	25	25	32
Full-time	2002	22	22	32
Full-time	2004	29	24	33
Part-time	2005	24	23	36
Full-time	2005	33	24	36
Part-time	2006	27	27	37
Full-time	2007	23	25	38
Part-time	2007	22	25	38
Full-time	2009	22	25	39

Source: Judicial Appointments Board for Scotland.

no reason why in the twenty-first century diversity should not be an integral part of merit, as indeed should geography. It is true that some have argued that being a judge is to be a skilled craftsperson in the same way as a surgeon. If there is no particular need for surgeons to reflect society, they say, why should there be for judges? Both parts of this argument are suspect. The now infamous MTAS reform in consultant recruitment in 2008 was introduced in part to encourage diversity in the profession, indeed, increased diversity in the professions has been government policy for a number of years now. As a result, one of the regulatory objectives of the Legal Services Acts in England and Scotland is the pursuit of diversity in the profession. Secondly, judges are *not* the same as surgeons. They are inescapably part of government and in a democracy governments have rightly concluded that they must be diverse.

Judicial selection

As is widely known, the judicial appointment mechanisms in the United Kingdom have been substantially reformed in the last decade. The old system of the Lord Chancellor or the Lord Advocate in Scotland appointing someone after consultation with the senior judiciary and others had certain advantages and it produced many excellent judges. However, it was wholly lacking in transparency, was not equal opportunities compliant, had no input from the non-lawyer community and was open to the accusation of cronyism. It was 'chaps appointing chaps'. So starting with Scotland and later in the rest of the United Kingdom, the Executive gave up its powers to appoint who it wanted as judges, leaving it instead to judicial appointment commissions. Judicial interest groups largely favoured this development, because, I suspect, they considered that if anyone was going to fill the power vacuum created by the Executive ceding its prerogative in this field, it should be the judiciary. This was a perfectly understandable position: they genuinely believed that they knew better than anyone what were the qualities required of a judge; that they should have the major say in the appointment process; and that this was in the public interest. Other stakeholders didn't entirely agree, seeing the potential for a democratic deficit being exacerbated rather than reduced through control of the appointment process. Not surprisingly there were tough negotiations between the Executive and the judiciary – the concordats I referred to earlier – as to what the composition of these appointment commissions should be. The judiciary would probably have preferred to have a judicial chair to the commissions, but succeeded only in Northern Ireland, in the rest of the United Kingdom it is a layperson. In England and Wales the lawyers and judges outnumber the lay members, in Scotland the Justice Minister of the time, Jim Wallace, bravely held out for a judicial appointment board that was 50 per cent lay and 50 per cent legal. Predictably, there have also been tensions over the definition of 'merit' and how diversity and geography is to fit into this. In short, the commissions have seen ongoing debates between its lay, legal and judicial members as to what the public interest as to judicial appointments requires and who should make those determinations. My own view is that the judicial appointment process is one of the few areas where accountability can be enhanced without threatening judicial independence, and that since the judiciary, and the senior judiciary in particular, are clearly a branch of government, democracy requires that the appointment process and the definition of 'merit' involves a strong and vigorous input from non-lawyers and that it should not be influenced disproportionately by the judiciary. I can do no better than to quote the wise words of Tom Legg, former Permanent Secretary in the Lord Chancellor's Department, and therefore responsible for hundreds of judicial appointments. He said with reference to the possible establishment of judicial appointment commissions: 'It is hard to imagine such [commissions] without a contingent of senior judges. They would inevitably have a heavy, and often a predominating, influence. It is no reflection on our judges to say that this would be undesirable. No branch of government should be effectively self-perpetuating.'[43]

Judicial appointment and the Supreme Court

What of Supreme Court appointments? Here, I would submit, the need for accountability is particularly strong. The eligibility criteria are very broad: any lawyer of fifteen years' standing is eligible to be appointed. This was the position with the House of Lords also, but when the 2005 Constitutional Reform Act was passed Parliament chose to retain the same breadth of eligibility. The process is by application submitted to an ad hoc

---

[43] T. Legg, 'Judges for the New Century', *Public Law* (2001), 62, 73. See also Robert Stevens: 'Judges do and should have political views. By giving the judges an even greater voice in the selection of their members than they have today, it is unclear why that should be superior from an apolitical point of view. It is replacing one oligarchy with another.' 'Unpacking the Judges', p. 20.

148

appointments commission whose Chair and Vice-Chair are the President and Deputy President of the Supreme Court, with one representative from each of the three permanent judicial appointment commissions, none of whom need be a woman and only one of whom need be a layperson.[44] The Commission interviews the short-listed applicants and consults with every Justice of the Supreme Court plus the senior judiciary (Lord Chief Justice, Master of the Rolls and the Divisional heads) and other significant stakeholders (the Lord Chancellor, the First Minister in Scotland and the First Minister in Wales)[45] about the suitability of the candidates. Appointment is on merit and a single name is offered to the Lord Chancellor for each vacancy. Unfortunately, this model has a number of drawbacks from an accountability perspective.

(1) First and foremost, it fails the Tom Legg /Robert Stevens 'self-perpetuating oligarchy'[46] test. Effectively, the Supreme Court is choosing its successors.[47] The critique is not personal to Lord Phillips and Lord Hope – it is an institutional problem.

---

[44] The *Report of the Advisory Panel on Judicial Diversity*, p. 41 suggested that there should always be a gender mix on the selection panel and if possible an ethnic mix. Curiously, the Panel had nothing to say about lay participation in the process.

[45] The Secretary of State for Northern Ireland was formerly a consultee, but with the devolution of justice and policing responsibilities the Secretary of State's role has now ceased. Instead, the Judicial Appointments Commission in Northern Ireland has to be consulted formally.

[46] Robert Stevens, *The English Judges* (Oxford: Hart Publishing, 2002), p. 177.

[47] The *Report of the Advisory Panel on Judicial Diversity*, Recommendation 41: 'No judge should be directly involved in the selection of his/her

(2) Secondly, the potential for a cloning effect is reinforced by the view, strongly held in certain quarters, that whatever the statute says, 'English and Welsh' positions on the Supreme Court should go to candidates who have served their time in the High Court and Court of Appeal.[48]

(3) Finally, the ad hoc panel has no obvious mechanism to deal with the situation where one of its members is faced with a serious conflict of interest in relation to a candidate, for example, a relative is an applicant.[49]

It is not easy to see how we can best solve some of these problems. If we accept that reverting to appointment by the Lord Chancellor is out of the question, then we will need another solution. Personally I would favour two

---

successor and there should always be a gender and, wherever possible, an ethnic mix on the selection panel.'

[48] See F. Gibb, 'Judges Oppose Appointment of Sumption QC to the Supreme Court', *The Times*, 15 October 2009 and F. Gibb, 'Supreme Ambition, Jealousy and Outrage', *The Times*, 4 February 2010. In this connection the appointment of a leading silk directly to the Supreme Court in 2011 is to be warmly welcomed. There seems no reason why brilliant city lawyers, academics or leaders of the Bar should not be appointable directly to the Court, as the earlier examples of Lords Reid and Radcliffe showed. The disinclination to appoint non-judicial candidates may also have diversity implications, given the dearth of female and ethnic minority judges in the higher courts. Interestingly, Lord Gardiner as Lord Chancellor believed in appointing Law Lords to the court with different philosophical perspectives. Similarly, Lord Phillips (the President of the Supreme Court) is of the opinion that there is a strong case for diversity in the recruitment of judges, including diversity of thought.

[49] In such a situation, it is difficult to see how a panellist could satisfy the *Porter* v. *Magill* [2001] UKHL 67 test without standing down.

innovations. As I have said, I believe it is abundantly clear that at the level of High Court and above the trickle-up theory is not working. It seems then that Kate Malleson may well be right to argue that a short-list of names should go to the Lord Chancellor with respect to any position from High Court and above and this short-list should contain at least one woman.[50] My second proposal is one that has received an airing from time to time: namely, that for appointments to the Supreme Court we should introduce a pre-appointment confirmation procedure appearance before a parliamentary select committee after nomination. The Lord Chief Justice has indicated his opposition to such a proposal,[51] as has the Lord Chancellor,[52] but it may be the least worst way of overcoming the democratic deficit that now confronts us.[53] The American public is far more aware as to the interests, values, expertise or track record of their most recent Supreme Court appointee than the British public is of ours. That is not a favourable comparison for us. Properly managed confirmation hearings can

---

[50] Kate Malleson, 'Is the Supreme Court a Constitutional Court in all but Name?', paper delivered at conference on 'The Supreme Court and the Constitution', Queen Mary University of London, 3 November 2010.

[51] Appearance before Constitutional Committee of the House of Lords, 15 December 2010.

[52] Appearance before Constitutional Committee of the House of Lords, 19 January 2011.

[53] See Mary Clark's helpful article, 'Introducing a Parliamentary Confirmation Process for new Supreme Court Justices', *Public Law* (2010), 464.

be informative without being intrusive or demeaning.[54] Accordingly, I would support a variant of such hearings in which candidates are asked politely by lawyers about their legal careers and outlook.

Greater disclosure and transparency

My third route to enhancing the accountability of the judiciary is to introduce greater measures of disclosure and transparency. Each and every justice of the US Supreme Court has to complete a detailed annual return setting out all their financial interests, including all shareholdings and offices held in other organisations. Moreover, when they have been nominated for appointment they are required to complete a very detailed questionnaire about their interests, publications and membership of organisations whether it be the masons, churches or golf clubs (single sex or otherwise).

Slightly surprisingly, the justices of the UK Supreme Court, who have rightly in my view been praised for being more transparent on a range of fronts than the House of Lords, have chosen on this front to be less transparent than they were in the House. In the House they were subject to a Register of Interests, but in February 2010[55] they indicated that they had

---

[54] In recent years confirmation hearings of Supreme Court justices in the United States have been fairly uneventful. Another model would be the public interview held with candidates for the South African Constitutional Court by a Judicial Selection Committee. See Kate Malleson, 'Selecting Judges in the Era of Devolution and Human Rights', in A. Le Sueur (ed.), *Building the UK's New Supreme Court* (Oxford University Press, 2004), p. 310.

[55] UKSC blog, 3 February 2010.

decided not to have a Register of Interests in the Supreme Court since (1) other judges in the United Kingdom do not have to complete a Register of Interests and (2) it would not be appropriate or indeed feasible for there to be a comprehensive register of the interests of all the justices. With the greatest of respect to the justices, I wonder if they have got this one right. The Supreme Court along with the rest of the (senior) judiciary is an arm of government, and democratic accountability normally means that we expect those who govern us to declare their interests – and not just on an as and when basis. A detailed Register of Interests might even have obviated the Pinochet affair.[56]

Recusal is a tricky area and I'm not sure that the answer is always to leave it to the judge who has been challenged to determine whether he or she has a disqualifying interest. I am confirmed in this line of thinking by Grant Hammond, the judicial author of what is now the leading textbook in the area.[57] The legal test is that laid down in *Porter v. Magill*:[58] namely, would the hypothetical, fair-minded, fully informed independent layperson having considered the facts conclude that there was a real possibility that the tribunal was biased. My difficulty is how the judges are to know the answer to that question. They cannot in the nature of things conduct

---

[56] *Pinochet, Re* [1999] UKHL 52, 15 January 1999. Where Lord Hoffmann failed to declare his involvement with a charity linked to Amnesty International, which was an intervener in the case. The tightening of the requirements of the House of Lords Register of Interest in recent years would almost certainly disclose such a link were it to arise today.

[57] Grant Hammond, *Judicial Recusal* (Oxford: Hart Publishing, 2009).

[58] [2002] 1 All E R 465 at para. 103 *per* Lord Hope.

an opinion poll survey. Here again, therefore, we are asking the judiciary to determine the public interest with very little to go on by way of objective evidence.

Another area where greater transparency and disclosure must surely be the way forward in the public interest lies in the appraisal of judges. I well remember in the early days of the Scots Judicial Appointments Board how one of the leading captains of industry received in blank amazement the information from one of the judicial members of the Board that judges in Scotland aren't subject to appraisal, and consider this to be in the interests of the public. Given that probably the most bizarre aspect of serving on that Board was that when part-time judges came before us seeking a full-time appointment there was no objective information whatsoever as to how well they had been performing as part-time judges, I have to say that I agree with the captain of industry. European judges accept appraisal by other judges as a perfectly normal aspect of judicial life and struggle to understand the allegation voiced by some in the United Kingdom that it threatens judicial independence. It follows also that I welcome the progress that has been made on this front in England and Wales.[59]

Next, we could benefit from greater transparency as to how judges are allocated to hear cases. I'm not sure that it was necessarily in the public interest that so many of the key decisions in the development of the law of privacy in recent years were made by the same High Court judge. At the level of the

---

[59] The *Advisory Panel on Judicial Diversity Report* in 2010 recommended that an appraisal system owned and run by the judiciary should be implemented to cover all levels within the judiciary (Recommendation 46).

House of Lords there was also a degree of misunderstanding as to the process by which members of panels in key appeals were selected. In fact, having interrogated several Principal Clerks of the House on this very matter over the last thirty-five years, I believe that it would have been helpful if there had been more transparency as to how the process worked. There was nothing untoward at all in what was done, but the lack of transparency hampered discussion of a matter which as time went by increasingly concerned some of the Law Lords – concerns which disclosure would probably largely have resolved.

Judicial decision-making

The final area of transparency and accountability that I propose to address is transparency in the appellate judicial decision-making process. As Robert Stevens observed: 'I can see advantages in encouraging the judges to be more open about their activities, for in the long run there are greater dangers to the democratic process by refusing to discuss the judicial process than by allowing reasoned articulation of the actual operation of the appeal courts.'[60]

In my original research on the Law Lords in the 1970s[61] I argued that, based on interviews with fifteen Law Lords and forty-six counsel, judicial decision-making in the Lords was a social and collective process but that this was not restricted to the interactions between the Law Lords. Rather,

---

[60] R. B. Stevens, 'The Role of a Final Appeal Court in a Democracy', *Modern Law Review*, 28 (1965), 509 at 539.
[61] A. Paterson, *The Law Lords* (London: Macmillan, 1982).

it was the product of a series of dialogues – some oral, some written, some symbolic, some real, with a whole range of stakeholders ranging from counsel to academics and Court of Appeal judges to Parliament. In 2008 with the assistance of the Nuffield Foundation, which I gratefully acknowledge, I embarked on a further round of forty-five interviews with Law Lords (twenty-two), Lord Justices (six) and others (seventeen) to see how the last Law Lords functioned. In what follows I should indicate my profound gratitude to the many Law Lords and others who over the years have endured my questioning with amazing tolerance and forbearing and to state that to the best of my belief what I'm about to relate has been cleared with the relevant interviewees from whom it came.

Some things hadn't changed in the House: the same committee rooms (Figure 4.2) with reporting back to the full chamber with a bishop present (Figure 4.3). The last case in the Lords was meant to be the delivery of the judgment in *Purdy*[62] – the assisted dying case – on Thursday, 30 July 2009, but on 31 July an urgent interlocutory matter arose in the *Jewish Free School* case. Not only did it give David Pannick QC his 100th appearance in the Lords, but when the Appeal Committee reported back to the Full Chamber they couldn't find a bishop to read the prayers. Fittingly, Lord Phillips, who has played many roles in his time, stood in for the missing bishop.

As for the research, I found that decision-making in the House of Lords still revolved around a series of dialogues,

---

[62] *Purdy, R (on the application of) v. Director of Public Prosecutions* [2009] UKHL 45, 30 July 2009.

Figure 4.2 An Appellate Committee chaired by Lord Hope, 2009

Figure 4.3   Lord Phillips giving judgment in the Chamber

but that the dialogues had changed. There were more of them, for example, with Judicial Assistants and foreign courts such as Strasbourg, thus subtly altering the tenor of the other dialogues. Moreover, the character of certain dialogues had changed both in type, for example, from oral to written, and also in significance.

With the Court of Appeal the dialogue had changed substantially in the last ten years as the latter became more and more vocal in their requests that the House should provide clearer guidance to lower courts. Matters came to a head in the *Doherty*[63] case, where Lord Justice Carnworth, ironically in a concurring judgment, chided the House in *Kay*[64] for giving six judgments with no clear majority ratio. As he subsequently put it, he had spent a weekend wrestling with a piece of self-assembly furniture, until he realised that IKEA had given him the wrong instructions leaflet. The problem with the House of Lords was that they had given him six different sets of instruction for the same case. Why couldn't the Law Lords issue a single judgment to make things clearer for the lower courts. The real irony of this case was that the majority in the *Kay* case, led by Lord Hope, had met three times to try to settle on their agreed ratio and they had agreed a joint paragraph,[65] and the Law Lords in *Doherty* met several times to try and improve on the paragraph, but interventions from Strasbourg indicated that the paragraph had not really settled the law. This was confirmed by the UK Supreme

---

[63] *Doherty v. Birmingham City Council* [2008] UKHL 57.
[64] *Kay v. Lambeth LBC* [2006] UKHL 10.
[65] Paragraph 110.

Court in the *Pinnock*[66] case in late 2010, in a judgment of the court[67] written with even further irony by the Master of the Rolls, Lord Neuberger, who had been one of Lord Justice Carnworth's companions in the *Doherty* appeal. Mark Twain said the difference between truth and fiction is that fiction has to be credible – how very true.

Law Lords and counsel

My recent interviews confirmed that the interface with counsel remained central to the decision-making process in the Lords, but that written arguments have doubled in size while oral ones have been halved in duration. This has had unexpected knock-on effects on the dialogue between the Law Lords themselves as we will see shortly. Lord Pannick QC,[68] described its unique atmosphere as a mixture of academic seminar, comfortable club and all-in wrestling match.[69] Lord Phillips, the last senior Law Lord told me:

[66] 2010 UKSC, 3 November 2010.

[67] Given the pre-history to the case it is likely to have involved much discussion between the justices even if only one author was credited with the judgment.

[68] In his valedictory column on the House in *The Times*, 30 July 2009. Lord Pannick was a veteran of 100 appearances in the House of Lords – the last of which was the final (and unscheduled) hearing in the Lords of a leave petition in the *Jewish Free School* case, which took place on Friday, 31 July, the day after the official end to judicial hearings in the court.

[69] The US Supreme Court in the last half century in contrast to the Bingham court, perhaps because of the severely curtailed periods of oral argument permitted there, has been described as 'designed as the Agincourt of the mind'. L. Baker, *Brandeis and Frankfurter, A Dual Biography* (New York: Harper & Row, 1984), p. 132.

> At its best the Lords work almost on a debating formula
> … it's a discussion in which the Lords and counsel are all
> taking part … I think the really good debater is the one
> who makes you feel that he's joining with you in seeking
> the right answer, whatever his point was. Of course he's
> not. [Laughter] But this is the secret of a really great
> advocate who makes you think that his only anxiety is to
> make sure you don't go wrong.

In Chapter 1 I addressed the question as to whether at the level of the Lords, advocacy really made a difference. Counsel and Law Lords differed on this issue, but not in a predictable way. Counsel were peculiarly modest as to the efficacy of their efforts. As Jonathan Sumption QC put it:

> I think that advocacy matters much more in perceiving
> what are likely to be regarded as the meritorious points,
> what are likely to be regarded as the direction the Lords
> will want to move in than in actually the analysis of
> case law or statutes … I don't think it ever makes the
> difference between success and failure but I think it makes
> a difference to the reasoning of a decision, which can be in
> the public interest.

Fortunately for counsel and their fee paying clients, the Law Lords were in general rather more positive as to the impact of good advocacy. All the Law Lords told me that they had changed their mind during the oral argument, and not that infrequently, in some cases. This was true thirty-five years ago and remains true today. They also considered that bad advocacy could lose cases in the Lords that should have been won.

Law Lords and Law Lords

The dialogues between the Law Lords and their fellow Law Lords were the most complex and subtle of all their dialogues. Clearly these were enduring in nature – some Law Lords had known each other since the date of their entry to the Bar. While such links did not mean that they thought alike on key legal and policy matters they did make it easier to drop into each other's rooms in the Law Lords' corridor to discuss the issues of the day. This aided decision-making in a myriad of ways: from suggesting lines of travel to be put to counsel, to testing the possible consequences of one outcome rather than another.[70] In specific appeals the dialogues would generally commence with consideration of the question of leave to appeal. By 2009 this was overwhelmingly a matter for the House of Lords rather than the Court of Appeal, since, as it was said, they preferred to dine *à la carte*. Normally, the decision to admit or not was made by an Appeal Committee comprising three Law Lords[71] with no input from the other Law Lords, which was an irritation

[70] It is easy to overlook the significance of the locations of judicial offices, which can inhibit dropping in on colleagues – as in the US Supreme Court – or reward those whose offices are located close to the secretaries and the coffee machine as was the case with the long Law Lords corridor. Indeed, there is an article to be written on the importance of geography for supreme courts: whether it be South Africa, where the Constitutional Court is located on the site of the former prison which once held Ghandi and Mandela, or the House of Lords, with its rather different symbolism.

[71] Very occasionally in the past, the senior Law Lord was more proactive and a phone call might be made to the Court of Appeal asking that leave be granted in a case.

to some. At one time there was a philosophy that any Law Lord could hear any type of case, but in the final years of the House, the Principal Clerk was running with the concept of 'A teams' for particular types of appeal, based on specialist background.[72] However, by that time also it was not unknown for some Law Lords, but by no means all, having heard that a particular appeal was on its way to the House, to ask the Principal Clerk if they could sit on that appeal since it raised a point of law in which they had a special interest. Where possible their name might well be included in the draft list of appeals and panels considered at a 'horses for courses' meeting with the two senior Law Lords once a term. Even latterly such requests were not the norm and a decade before such requests were virtually unknown.[73]

The papers for appeals were provided to the Law Lords some weeks before the date for the Appellate Committee. Yet in the 1970s most of the heavyweight Law Lords of the time, Reid, Radcliffe, Denning and Devlin, read them very sparingly if at all, knowing it would all come out in the oral hearing.[74] In the modern era with printed Cases having doubled in size and oral argumentation halved from four to two days all the Law Lords read in advance, although to varying degrees, and counsel were expected to present their arguments with that in

---

[72] Although not a lawyer the Clerk elicited from senior Law Lords and from new Law Lords ideas as to their legal specialisms and interests and from this evolved his idea of 'A teams'. This was not a foolproof process, and in any event other factors would come in to disrupt the proposed composition of a panel.

[73] Brice Dickson, 'The Processing of Appeals in the House of Lords', Law Quarterly Review, 123 (2007), 571–601.

[74] See Paterson, The Law Lords.

mind. Dealing with a panel with different stages of prepared-ness – known in the United States as a lukewarm bench – posed peculiar challenges to counsel.

In terms of oral dialogue, in Lord Reid's era there were constant exchanges between the Law Lords throughout the hearing of the appeal. They would chat in the library before the start of an appeal, interact with each other in the guise of asking questions to counsel, talk together at lunch in the Peer's Dining Room and at the end of the day's hearing lean-ing against the wall in the corridor. In direct contrast to the lengthy arguments from counsel, these debates were highly compressed – almost in shorthand:[75] 'But if you say that, then it leads to [such and such] consequences', or somebody says 'No, because in that case …'[76]

The sheer length of oral argumentation in Lord Reid's era – four days on average[77] (although the *Tin Mines* case

---

[75] Paterson, *The Law Lords*, p. 91

[76] As one of them put it: 'You break off say at four o'clock, then starts the argument. Three people arguing, then up drifts a fourth, and you really thrash the thing out. Then somebody raises a point which you think you can demolish … [Since] you want to convince them that the other point is right, you look at a Law Report when you come in, in the morning beforehand, and casually remark as you gather in the library for a quarter of an hour, that it seems to you that the case of so-and-so really has got the right principle much more. Then the argument starts again' (Paterson, *The Law Lords*, p. 91).

[77] In the early 1970s (derived from my tables from original research). Between 1952 and 1968 25 per cent of English appeals to the Lords lasted more than five days and 10 per cent of them took seven days or more. L. Blom-Cooper and G. Drewry, *Final Appeal* (Oxford: Clarendon Press, 1972), p. 235.

weighed in at a staggering twenty-six days)[78] – meant that the oral exchanges with their colleagues during a case were extensive, changes of mind at this stage were commonplace, and by the end of the appeal most people knew where everyone else stood. But by 2009 the Law Lords did not discuss cases much in advance with each other (although a few did with their judicial assistants), did not lunch altogether or discuss cases very much at lunch and with shorter hearings had fewer opportunities to engage with their colleagues or elicit the views of the more silent ones such as Lord Nicholls or Lord Walker.

The conference at the end of hearings appears not to have changed very much in character over the last forty or so years. Typically, it lasted for no more than an hour (although they could range from half an hour to half a day),[79] which is rather shorter than in the US Supreme Court.[80] It usually started as soon as the oral hearing had ended, with the Law Lords delivering their off-the-cuff views on the appeal in order from the most junior to the most senior, the reverse order from the US Supreme Court. Contributions came with varying degrees of tentativeness. Interestingly, some saw it as their best chance for judicial advocacy and would prepare for it accordingly. Others did not. Most of this conference consisted of a seriatim presentation of views with little interruption

---

[78] *J. H. Rayner Ltd* v. *Department of Trade and Industry & Others* [1990] 2 AC 418.

[79] Paterson, *The Law Lords*, p. 94: *Ross Smith* lasted half a day and *Heaton's Transport* a whole day.

[80] This too varies: conferences under Rehnquist CJ were shorter than those under Roberts CJ. The latter preferring time for an exchange of views in the hope of consensus-building, the former considering that there was little point.

and no one speaking twice until all had spoken once. Actual debates or discussions of the issues in the case tended not to be lengthy except in the occasional especially important or complex appeal, where by planning in advance a morning had been set aside for the conference. In the great bulk of cases the first conference was the only collective discussion between the panel.[81] (The *Kay* and *Doherty* cases were quite unusual in this respect.) Once the conference was over, if all were agreed on the result it would usually be decided who would write the main or lead opinion, and who would deal with the facts. Within a week or so the Law Lords would start to circulate their draft judgments and final judgments would be promulgated within six to eight weeks of the hearing,[82] again considerably faster than in the US Supreme Court.

To sum up, although the types of dialogue between the Law Lords themselves have remained fundamentally the same over the last forty years, there have been several changes. Taken together, these sometimes subtle alterations in the Law Lords' practices meant that by the end in 2009 the character of

---

[81] Occasionally, if time was pressing and the Law Lords were split the conference would be adjourned to later in the week.

[82] Between 1952 and 1968 it was said to be six weeks: Blom-Cooper and Drewry, *Final Appeal*, p. 236. At the millennium, however, the circulation of opinions among the Law Lords had become a drawn-out process typically exceeding three months and sometimes taking more than eight months. In 2000 the average delay between hearing and judgment was ninety-five days, with two cases taking more than 250 days and a further two taking a year. Partly as a result of Lord Bingham's arrival in the final decade of the House, the average gap from hearing to promulgation dropped to less than two months, with very few taking more than five months.

these exchanges was different. From a decision-making process forty years ago that used to be largely oral, it had become one that was significantly more in writing.[83]

So far, so bland, but what was decision-making really like? Were the Law Lords all cast from the same mould. Of course not. Nor were their views of the role. Lord Goff once said, 'A crumb of analysis is worth a whole loaf of opinion.'[84] So let me try to analyse what has been happening. Some Law Lords saw themselves as part of a collegial body, which at its best would arrive at decisions through a process of consensus-building. Others were more tactically inclined, recognising that typically all they required was to garner two supporting votes to achieve a majority position in the case. As Lord Hoffmann told me: 'I don't think of it as a collective [process], I think of it as a situation in which you want two other votes … that's what you've got to do.' Twenty years earlier one of his predecessors wryly observed:

> If I can influence or control the majority, it is not worthwhile arguing [the dissenters] round. It merely tires them and tires me. I think it was Disraeli who said, 'A majority is the best repartee'.

At the other end of the spectrum were the soloists, who for whatever reason favoured a more individual decision-making approach to a more collective process. Collegiality as a model of judicial decision-making is making some explanatory

---

[83] There was a short-lived era in the middle when Lord Diplock was senior Law Lord and single judgments became the norm and oral discussion increased as a result.

[84] *Hunter and Others v. Canary Wharf Ltd* [1997] AC 655 at 694.

headway in the panoply of theories of judicial behaviour that have emerged from Northern America in recent times.[85] The term does not refer to how well the court's members get on with each other, but to how much they work together as a team pursuing a common enterprise and how much they function as individuals. The English Court of Appeal is a highly collegial court. Its members regularly sit in the same panel for several weeks, they meet before cases to discuss points on which they wish to hear argument, to allocate who will write and to express preliminary views on the case. There may be subsequent meetings when the opinion has been circulated. The sheer pressure of business coupled with the need to play to the specialist strengths within each panel only emphasises their inter-dependence and the necessity for team playing.

It must be doubted if the House was ever as collegial as that – and it certainly was not in its final decade. Nevertheless, in terms of the spectrum of individualism to collegiality, most recent Law Lords were somewhere in the middle. Most thought it perfectly appropriate to seek to influence a colleague, where they differed was over how this might best be done – in writing, orally, in person or in a group context. There were also differences as to the stage in the process when it could most advantageously be done. Lord Hoffmann used his exchanges with counsel to make points to his colleagues:[86]

---

[85] See H. T. Edwards, 'The Effects of Collegiality on Judicial Decision-Making', *University of Pennsylvania Law Review*, 151 (2003), 1639.

[86] Lord Scott appears to have used his interventions for a similar purpose, but since his take on cases was frequently slightly different from that of some of his colleagues the interventions did not always have their intended effect.

> That is the stage at which you make your view known
> both for benefit of counsel and for the benefit of your
> colleagues. It's an opportunity not just for counsel to
> exercise advocacy on the bench but for the judges to
> exercise advocacy on each other.

Lord Hoffmann extended his judicial advocacy into the first conference,[87] but thereafter his efforts switched to writing, hoping to have an impact by a very early circulation of his opinion. This tactic could irk a few of his colleagues and amuse others if it emerged more or less with the end of the hearing.[88] Even if his tactics occasionally misfired, Lord Hoffmann was a formidable colleague who had some notable successes in winning round his fellows through the circulation of his judgment, *R v. BBC, ex p. Pro Life Alliance*[89] being perhaps the best known. Like Lords Reid and Radcliffe before him, Lord Hoffmann thought that lobbying his colleagues at the circulation stage was pointless: if you couldn't win them over by your written argument you weren't going to succeed by going to their rooms.

Collegiality has an interesting interface with concurring and dissenting judgments, as James Lee charmingly

---

[87] It is not the practice to interrupt a Law Lord's statement of his or her views at the conference unless the presentation contains a factual error or a misunderstanding of what an earlier (and more junior) Law Lord had said.

[88] Writing and circulating very late can equally prove counter-productive as some Law Lords found to their cost. Lord Goff took so long to draft the lead opinion in a case that by the time he had done so Lord Hoffmann had changed his vote to the other side.

[89] [2003] UKHL 23, 10 April 2003.

illustrates in 'A Defence of Concurring Speeches'.[90] The acme of collegiality is the single judgment of the court as practised in many European courts including *the* European Court and the European Court of Human Rights. It was also practised in the Privy Council, but not in the House. Despite this, in the politically charged case of *Heatons Transport* [91] in 1972 Lord Wilberforce managed to adopt the formula of a judgment of the court. Unfortunately, a scrutiny of the Minute Book provides no explanation as to how this sleight of hand had been achieved. Many years later, Lord Bingham, who had been a counsel in the *Heatons* case, remembered the event and persuaded the Principal Clerk that the Appellate Committee in the case of *R* v. *Forbes*[92] could have a single report of the Committee. In the ensuing eight years the House repeated the ploy twenty-three times out of 510 appeals[93] in cases where Lord Bingham and his colleagues felt that the need for certainty in the criminal law required the statement of the law with a single voice. However, in general, Lord Bingham – despite the Court of Appeal's IKEA moments – did not feel that the lack of a single judgment of the court was problematic in collegial terms, provided the ratio from multiple speeches was clear and the limits of appropriate judicial law-making were adhered to, especially in criminal law.[94] Indeed, as James

---

[90] *Public Law* (2009), 305.
[91] *Heatons Transport (St Helens) Ltd* v. *Transport and General Workers Union* [1973] AC 15.
[92] [2001] 1 AC 473.
[93] See Lee, 'A Defence of Concurring Speeches', p. 311.
[94] See Lord Bingham, 'The Rule of Law', *Cambridge Law Journal*, 66 (2007), 67, 70–1 and *The Rule of Law*, p. 45.

Lee has argued,[95] concurring opinions serve dissenting, buttressing and mediating functions, all of which can be collegial in nature. 'Dissenting' concurrences providing a 'misleading patina of harmony'[96] as to the result but not the reasons, do not seem very collegial. Yet collegial Law Lords in the last decade from time to time practised something very similar: namely, the 'tactical assent' designed to encourage the majority to adopt a somewhat different principle than they originally intended. One instance of this appears to have been Lady Hale's speech in *AL (Serbia)* v. *Secretary of State for Home Department*.[97]

Dissent was 160 per cent less common in the House than in the US Supreme Court (Figures 4.4 and 4.5). Maybe sitting in large panels has an impact on the issue – we shall see. However, although out and out dissents do not seem very collegial, curiously where a Law Lord fell on the spectrum of individualism to collegiality was not necessarily reflected in a propensity to dissent and vice versa. Of course, some high dissenters were individualists by inclination such as Lord Keith (the father) and Lord Guest with dissent rates of 16 per cent and 9 per cent, respectively, but Lord Denning who dissented in 15 per cent of appeals while in the Lords tried to be collegial, but generally found his brethren reluctant to agree with him.[98] Similarly, Lord Radcliffe, also with a high dissent rate (9 per cent), was described by Lord Wilberforce as an intellectually

[95] See Lee, 'A Defence of Concurring Speeches'.
[96] See Lee, 'A Defence of Concurring Speeches', p. 318.
[97] [2008] UKHL 42.
[98] See Paterson, *The Law Lords*, p. 112.

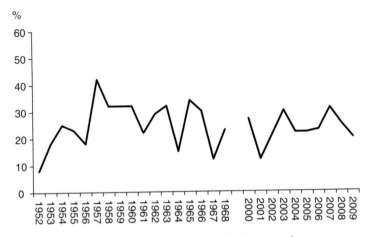

Figure 4.4   Proportion of cases with a dissent in the
House of Lords 1952–68 and 2000–9
Source: House of Lords.

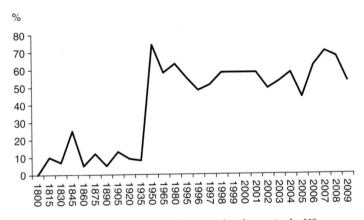

Figure 4.5   Proportion of cases with a dissent in the US
Supreme Court 1800–2009
Source: US Supreme Court.

brilliant judge, but lacking in the power to persuade his colleagues. In truth, there is a difference between dissenting on your own and dissenting with others. The former is often an individualist act, the latter is not. Over the last forty years a significant minority of Law Lords have not thought it worthwhile to dissent on their own unless it was on a point of principle. In the last decade alone the Law Lords have been twice as likely to dissent with a colleague rather than to dissent on their own.[99] Dissenting with a colleague, however, is not simply to set a marker for the future, it is also to send a marker for the present.[100] It may even induce one of the majority to swing over (Figure 4.6). Dissenting with others, therefore, is often a collegial response.

Even this analysis of dissents in the Lords oversimplifies matters. This is because dissents have to be broken down further. While 11 per cent of appeals in the Lords between 1952 and 1968 and 2000 and 2009 were sole dissents, they were of two different types. Those where the dissenter was isolated from an early stage,[101] for example, Lord Bingham in his later dissents,[102] and those where a Law Lord started out with one

---

[99] The latter as Lord Ackner put it, are occasions where the Law Lord's outrage at the majority's position overcomes their natural indolence.

[100] For example, it may be used to send a message to the Government that it may have won this case, but that it had only squeaked home by 3:2.

[101] Their dissent could be triggered by the collegial consensus of the rest of the panel. See Edwards, 'The Effects of Collegiality on Judicial Decision-Making', on dissent and collegiality.

[102] *Secretary of State for Defence* v. *Al-Skeini & Others* [2007] UKHL 26, 13 June 2007; *Countryside Alliance and others, R (on the application of)* v. *Attorney General & Another* [2007] UKHL 52, 28 November 2007;

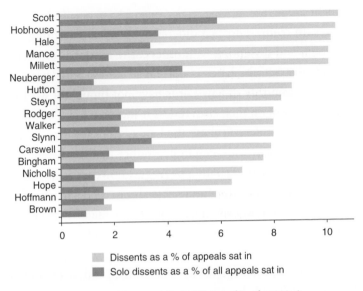

Figure 4.6   Dissenters in the House of Lords 2000–9
Source: House of Lords.

or more colleagues, like Lord Walker in the *Belmarsh* case or Lord Neuberger in *Stack and Dowden*[103] only to find that when the dust had settled and vote switching was over, they were on their own as the sole dissenter. To treat the latter dissenters as individualists because they didn't withdraw their opinion and align themselves with the rest seems analytically dubious. Similarly, finely balanced cases (3:2, 4:3 or 5:4) which made up a further 11 per cent of appeals in the Lords between 1952 and 1968 and 2000 and 2009 fell into three categories. Those where

Chief Constable of the Hertfordshire Police v. *Van Colle; Smith* v. *Chief Constable of Sussex Police* [2008] UKHL 50, 30 July 2008.

[103] [2007] UKHL 17, 25 April 2007.

the minority Law Lords were formerly part of the majority but ended up in the minority through late vote switches; those where there was only ever one swing voter; and those where nobody was in any doubt about their position at any stage in the case. What this shows is that to categorise cases by their outcome (and Law Lords by their final position in a case) is to sometimes underplay the dynamic process by which the outcome was achieved. Law Lords who started out thinking that they were writing the lead opinion occasionally found that due to vote switches they were now a dissenter.

Finely balanced cases were disliked by some of the Law Lords I talked to this time round, since on one view they are evidence that in these cases at least a differently composed panel of Law Lords might have reached a different conclusion.[104] Usually, this was a reference to the divergent perspectives and policy preferences of different Law Lords. However, sometimes the outcome of finely balanced cases was determined, as Lord Wilberforce argued, by the ability of some of the Law Lords in the Committee to influence some of their colleagues in a particular direction. Here it may be of some relevance that an analysis of the voting records of Law Lords in the last decade shows that some Law Lords, including Lords Bingham, Brown, Hoffmann, Hope and Millett were twice as likely to be in the majority side of a 3:2 or 4:3 split as on the minority side. Of course, that does not tell us if they were

---

[104] In *White* v. *Chief Constable of South Yorkshire Police* [1999] 1 All ER 1 at 40, Lord Hoffmann referred to *McLaughlin* v. *O'Brien* [1983] 1 AC 410 as 'one of those cases in which one feels that a slight change in the composition of the Appellate Committee would have set the law on a different course'.

leaders or followers. The answer to that question, as well as to which of the more recent Law Lords were of which disposition on the individualism to collegiality spectrum will have to await another occasion.

However, let me illustrate my argument by drawing a contrast between two senior Law Lords who in different ways had a very significant impact on the House as a final court of appeal and on their colleagues. I refer to Lords Diplock and Bingham. Each occupied a different place on the spectrum of individualism to consensus-building, but each had a huge impact on their colleagues and the court.

(1) *The hearings.* At the stage of the dialogue with counsel the two could not have been more different. Lord Diplock, who prepared ferociously for cases at a time when most of his colleagues did not, would discuss the appeal in advance with his colleagues to ascertain their views. He had no truck with a measured exposition of the principal arguments in the case, and would bully counsel who could not stand up to him in order to speed up the hearing. Lord Bingham, when he arrived in the House found that a tradition had grown up of not discussing cases prior to the hearing, contrary to the practice in the Court of Appeal.[105] The tradition was a reaction to the perceived dangers of forceful presiders such as Lord Diplock pushing the court in a preferred direction too early. Lord Bingham came to see the value of this tradition for keeping minds open for as long as possible, and maintained the

---

[105] There were a few exceptional cases where the members of the Appellate Committee would meet before the hearing where there was some problem that had to be dealt with.

tradition, though his successor Lord Phillips was not alone in seeing the merits of the Court of Appeal practice of meeting in advance to identify areas of difficulty for counsel to focus on.[106] Lord Bingham kept counsel's arguments moving on by the use of the clipped 'Yes', and made them adhere to their time estimates, but otherwise was considered a model presider for allowing counsel time to set out their stall in a relatively uninterrupted way. The respect which his colleagues had for him prevented even the impatient ones from trying to cut short counsel.[107]

(2) *The first conference.* History does not record how Lord Diplock ran the first conference when he presided,[108]

---

[106] Lord Phillips when he took over as senior Law Lord had a different view: 'In an ideal world I think there would be an advantage in our meeting well beforehand having read at least each side's case, the statement of facts and issues in order to see which issues we found most difficult and where we thought the problems were going to arise. Then one could inform counsel that we would particularly like help on this or on that. Having discussed the difficult areas the Law Lord in the chair would know that he could push the counsel along quickly through areas where we didn't really feel we needed help. At the moment if you don't know what your colleagues are interested in, there's a reluctance to say, "Oh you needn't bother with that, get on to the next one," because you don't know whether he does need to bother with that' (Interview with author).

[107] When Lord Bingham was not in the chair, the position could be different. See Lord Hope's account of Lord Hoffmann's curtailment of the arguments in the Pitcairn Islands case *Christian and Others* v. *The Queen* [2006] UKPC 47 in the Foreword to Dawn Oliver (ed.), *Justice, Legality and the Rule of Law* (Oxford University Press, 2009).

[108] Regrettably, although a clerk from the Judicial Office was present throughout all first conferences in the House, nothing of the proceedings appears in the Minute Book.

however, since he is reputed not infrequently to have written his judgment before the end of the hearing we can be sure that he had a clear view as to the outcome which he favoured for the case. As Lord Wilberforce subsequently observed:

> I think that as a general point you cannot really estimate a judge's influence without knowing from behind the scenes what influence he had on his colleagues ... Lord Diplock possessed the quality of persuading his colleagues to the extreme ... it almost got to the stage of a mesmeric quality ... He was a man who got his way in almost everything ... He would work on persuading people to his point of view during the conduct of a case, in the lunch intervals, in the corridors, in their rooms. I do not know anybody else who had this ability, and the desire to exercise it, so strongly as he did. Lord Diplock was a very persuasive man.[109]

Clearly, Lord Diplock was towards the tactician end of the spectrum, what the small group analysts label as a 'task leader'.[110] Clearly, too, he will have used the conference to persuade wavering colleagues. In one respect, however, Lord Diplock must have envied his counterpart in the US Supreme Court. There the Chief Justice speaks first at the conference. This is a real opportunity for judicial advocacy. Rehnquist is reputed not to have taken advantage of the opportunity – being of the opinion that by the stage of the conference the justices would have made up their minds. Chief Justice Roberts, however, undoubtedly does, seeing it as a huge opportunity

---

[109] Quoted in G. Sturgess and P. Chubb, *Judging the World* (Sydney: Butterworths, 1988), p. 275.

[110] See Paterson, *The Law Lords*, pp. 110 and 116.

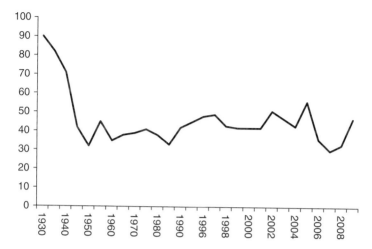

Figure 4.7   Unanimous decisions in the US Supreme Court
1930–2009
Source: US Supreme Court.

to re-frame the issues to fit his vision of the case. In his first
year as Chief Justice he consciously pursued the objective of
consensus-building in the court through framing the issues
in appeals in as narrow a way as possible, thereby achieving a
substantial increase in unanimous decisions. Such tactics can
reduce the value of decisions from the final court of appeal
and not surprisingly the percentage of unanimous cases has
fallen again[111] (Figure 4.7).

[111] In 2005, under the leadership of Chief Justice Roberts, 56 per cent of
decisions of the US Supreme Court were unanimous. The percentage
of unanimous decisions fell to 30 per cent in 2007, but rose to 46 per
cent in 2009. For a critical article on the downsides of pursuing a faux
unanimity – it fails to provide clear guidance to the lower courts – see
Adam Liptak, 'Justices are Long on Words but Short on Guidance', *New
York Times*, 17 November 2010.

Typically, Lord Bingham's approach was quite different. Like Lord Hoffmann he saw the first conference as an opportunity for judicial advocacy, but not for him, but for the junior Law Lord who spoke first. As he remarked:

> I think it's rather a good feature of the system that those who are newest and most junior do have this rather important role because otherwise they may wonder why they're there at all [laughs]. So I've encouraged them to address the subject quite fully and that means that everybody else tends to be a good deal briefer because they'll say 'Well I agree with him on this and I'll agree with her on that' or 'I agree completely with what X has said and I'll therefore give my own reasons very briefly'.

Of course, despite Tom's generosity it made no difference to his influence when it came to his turn to speak. Several of his colleagues recalled how not infrequently when the Committee was divided or occasionally even when it was not, the sheer force of his intellect and the clarity of his thinking would win his colleagues round.[112] But Bingham was not a tactician or a consensus-builder or an individualist. He was in the middle. He did seek to persuade his colleagues at the first conference and with his circulated opinion but not in the way that Lord Diplock did. 'He led by example and persuasion rather than necessarily setting out to do it', observed one colleague.

---

[112] 'It is not unknown to hear four views going one way, and then to hear Lord Bingham going the other way, after which the four eventually decide to come round to Lord Bingham's point of view', Lady Hale, in 'A Supreme Judicial Leader', M. Andenas and Fairgrieve (eds.), *Tom Bingham and the Transformation of the Law* (2009), p. 219.

'He carried terrific weight always and through sheer intellectual ability', said another, but he didn't throw his weight about. It was said of Lord Reid that 'When counsel had concluded their submissions, the time came for each of us, in conference, to outline his own provisional position. After Reid, speaking last, had given his opinion, one was left with the feeling, not so much that any other conclusion would be wrong in law, as it would be inadequate. The whole implications, often wider than the point in dispute, had been assembled and dealt with … Not only a judge, but a statesman was speaking.'[113] Lord Bingham's colleagues felt much the same about him.

However, sometimes Lord Bingham's opportunity was lost. In one 3:2 case – let's call it *A* v. *B* – the conference at 4 pm had to be cut short because people had something else to go to. It was clear there was a split in the court and even who the swing voter might be but not which way that person would go, and Lord Bingham didn't have the opportunity to definitely win over the waverer. Being Tom he left it there, Lord Diplock would never have done that.

(3) *Opinion assignment*. At the end of the first conference Lord Diplock would assign the lead opinion, often to himself. As is well known, Lord Diplock was a firm believer that there should be more single judgments and being a very persuasive man he got his way, with single judgments in the House peaking at 68 per cent in 1985. This did not survive for long after his death in harness in 1985. Lord Bingham was of a different persuasion as we have seen. Apart from a few

---

[113] A. Paterson, 'Scottish Lords of Appeal 1876–1988', *The Juridical Review* (1988), 235, 251.

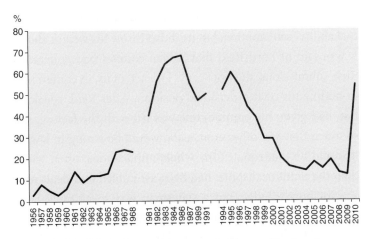

Figure 4.8   Single judgments in the House of Lords and
Supreme Court 1952–2010
Source: House of Lords research and Supreme Court web site.

criminal appeals he favoured multiple opinions, like Lord
Reid before him, provided efforts were made to secure a clear
majority ratio and the limits of judicial law-making were
observed. In the great bulk of cases Lord Bingham's view was
to allow anyone who wished to write or to dissent. During his
era single judgments in the House dropped to around 18 per
cent of cases. However, the position as to single judgments has
changed dramatically with the advent of the Supreme Court.
In its first year 55 per cent of its cases have been determined
with a single judgment (Figure 4.8).

The atmosphere of laissez faire meant that there was
relatively little bargaining or negotiation over the content of the
Law Lords' individual opinions in the last decade as compared
with the US Supreme Court. The recent dramatic increase in
single judgments in the UK Supreme Court is likely to lead

to more such discussions, but did not do so initially. The odd occasions when a presiding Law Lord had to reconvene the members of panel after the circulation of the judgments came about because no clear ratio or principle of the decision was emerging from the majority judgments. This, it will be recalled was one of Lord Bingham's caveats for allowing multiple judgments. This occurred in *Common Services Agency* v. *Scottish Information Commissioner (Scotland).*[114] After the circulation there were five divergent judgments all for the same result, and this in what the presider, Lord Hoffmann regarded as a straightforward case. He called a meeting and eventually it was agreed that he and Lord Mance would withdraw their judgments and that Lord Hope would adjust the wording of his opinion to take account of their suggestions.

As to the allocation of the facts[115] Lord Bingham told me:

> I always tried to decide who was going to write the facts because it seemed to me almost mischievous for everybody to have a go ... so that I did try to achieve a position where we went out of the committee room knowing who was going to do the facts and encouraging everybody else to leave them alone, but one wasn't always successful in that.

[114] [2008] UKHL 47, 9 July 2008.

[115] Where there is a lead opinion it will also deal with the facts. But even where there is no lead opinion someone has to be responsible for the facts. In the US Supreme Court assigning the lead opinion is far more important, since that court requires a majority opinion if it is to have effect as a precedent. This has allowed successive Chief Justices to use the allocation power tactically. However, if the Chief Justice is in the minority the power of allocation falls to the most senior justice in the majority.

Interestingly, Lord Bingham would allocate who was to write the facts whichever side he was on, unless he thought the majority side was really misguided, as he said to me:

> I think if I was in the minority I might still want to do the facts myself [laughs] not with a view to putting a slant on them ... but because ... other things being equal its quite good to get the facts at the beginning of five opinions ... [rather] than later on. Sometimes, [however] I would feel that it was up to the majority to organise how they were going to organise their opinions. [Thus] in cases where one just flatly disagreed with what the majority were agreeing ... one would rather say 'Well, how you're going to construct your house is a matter for you and not me'.

(4) *The circulation of judgments*. We've heard about Lord Diplock's writing habits. What about Lord Bingham's? Tom Bingham wrote very quickly indeed – he was celebrated for it by his colleagues – as he put it:

> Well Alan Rodger slightly teased me with having never grown out of writing a weekly essay [laughs] and there is actually truth in that. My regime over the last eight years ... was a very, very clear routine. One would sit in court on Monday to Thursday, Thursday night we would go down to our house in the country where I have quite a considerable law library and I'd take all the papers and the cases with me and then Friday, Saturday, Sunday I would write my opinion and get it typed up on Monday and then circulate it.

Unlike Lord Hoffmann, who usually circulated at a very early stage in an attempt to influence his colleagues, Lord Bingham produced his 300 manuscript pages a weekend, because that was how he liked to work – he wanted to get the thing off his desk before he was into another case. He was congenitally incapable of sitting on an opinion unless it was a truly exceptional case such as *Belmarsh*. Although he recognised that it was a weakness he had a great reluctance to revisit an opinion which he had circulated some time before.[116] If he was writing what he thought was to be the leading opinion he would entertain his colleagues' requests for tweaks here or dropping a phrase there. But if he was not he was reluctant to comment on others' opinions even where he thought they were misconceived, because he considered judicial independence involved independence from one's colleagues.

As he explained:

> I think they have an expression in the Supreme Court
> in the United States, 'creeping around the hall' which is
> all the law clerks going off and lobbying the law clerks of
> other justices to try and build coalitions … Well, our law
> clerks don't do that at all but nor do the members mostly.
> Some do, but I myself absolutely never did. If people didn't
> agree with me, they didn't agree with me, but I wasn't
> going to indulge in 'robing room advocacy' to try and get
> them to change their mind.

Here, therefore, we can see that Lord Bingham was not a tactician and generally not an intentional consensus-builder,[117] if he didn't win his colleagues over at the first conference or with

---

[116] One case in which he did was *R v. Rahman* [2008] UKHL 45, but he didn't change his position and as a result ended up in a 3:2 minority on a sub-issue in the case.

[117] Except where there were judgments of the court.

the circulated opinion, that was largely it. In this respect, as we have seen, he was not very far apart from Lords Hoffmann, Reid and Radcliffe. Occasionally, this had its downsides. Tom lost the *A* v. *B* case, which he felt strongly about because of the truncated first conference and his disinclination to counter the efforts of the majority Law Lords to persuade the swing voter to stay with them. Again, the judgments in *Smith* v. *Chief Constable of Sussex*[118] suggest that two of his colleagues might have been persuaded had he taken the opportunity to push his position beyond the first circulation.

Lord Diplock, we know, would have had no such scruples. Nor curiously, would Lord Wilberforce. The latter told me:

> One learns to one's surprise that some people who are thought of as wonderful judges are lacking in the art of persuading their colleagues to adopt their point of view. Whereas others who are not much on the record in print are extremely good at directing a decision in a particular way.

Lord Wilberforce's observation appeared directed at non-tacticians, in fact it held true also for tacticians who were ineffective. For example, Lord Atkin lobbied his colleagues regularly, but was not open to persuasion in return, which irked them and reduced his efficacy on the court.[119] Viscount Simonds also disliked losing or even losing the vote of a colleague whom he respected, and would hold several meetings to try to achieve consensus. Judged by the outcome of the 3:2 cases in which he

---

[118] [2008] UKHL 50, 30 July 2008.
[119] Paterson, *The Law Lords*, p. 117.

found himself his efforts at 'task leadership' to win round his colleagues were not especially successful.[120]

To set against this there have been many examples of effective task leadership over the years in the Lords. Lord Devlin turning his colleagues in *Rookes* v. *Barnard*;[121] Lord Griffiths doing the same in *Pepper* v. *Hart*[122] after the first hearing of that celebrated appeal; Lord Hoffmann staring a 4:1 defeat in the face after the first conference in *R* v. *BBC, ex p. Pro Life Alliance*[123] swinging all but one round by the end; and *Stack* v. *Dowden*,[124] where sufficient votes are thought to have swung to change the majority position in the case.

Belmarsh

I have been arguing that transparency in appellate decision-making aids accountability. Let me offer one last example. Although there were many highlights in the era of the Bingham court this case can lay claim to being the greatest. Lord Bingham certainly regarded it as the most important case that he had to decide in his career and assigned nine Law Lords to hear it. It concerned whether the detention without trial of foreign nationals suspected of terrorism was compatible with the Human Rights Act. Although there had been earlier challenges to the Government under the Act, Lord Bingham felt that this was the first serious challenge

[120] Paterson, *The Law Lords*, p. 120.
[121] *(No. 1)* [1964] UKHL 1.
[122] [1992] UKHL 3, 26 November 1992.
[123] [2003] UKHL 23, 10 April 2003.
[124] [2007] UKHL 17 para. 14.

to the Government's anti-terrorism strategy to come to the House, and he wanted the House to do it justice. Rather than take the case in July when energies were flagging, Tom opted instead for an October hearing – a decision he subsequently regretted. To the neutral observer the sides were evenly balanced at the end of the hearing and indeed they were. A particularly powerful submission for the Secretary of State swung some votes in the Government's direction and at the end of the first conference the vote was only 5:4 against the Government. Unfortunately, no special provision had been built in for writing time and almost uniquely in his tenure in the House, Lord Bingham's schedule did not permit him to write his opinion for nearly six weeks. With Lord Steyn recused the mantle for circulating quickly would normally have fallen to Lord Hoffmann, but perhaps because his mind was moving in the direction of his ultimate 'dissent' it is not clear that he was first into print. Lord Walker did probably get his out early, but he was not in the majority. The two Scots came out powerfully for the majority and gradually the votes won by the Government's submissions slowly eked away. Lord Carswell's views, which had moved about a bit in the case, came down against the Government and Lord Walker found himself in a minority of one, which had not been the position at any of the earlier stages in the appeal. At the end of the hearing Lord Bingham had indicated that he would write and deal with the facts and whether it was the first to be written or not, his judgment by tradition was the first to be delivered in the Chamber of the House and also in the Law Reports. Inevitably, posterity has come to see it as the lead judgment. Although Lord Bingham's prose was as pellucid as ever, his tone as one former colleague put it, was flat as a pancake. This was a deliberate strategy on Tom's part. As he recalled later:

> My opinion in *Belmarsh* was very deliberately written in very low key and extremely uninflammatory language with no big rhetorical high spots because one knew perfectly well it was going to be extremely unpopular with the powers that be. I didn't want it to sound like a political speech of a hostile kind so I myself made a clear decision to make it very low key and unrhetorical in tone … My recollection is that when delivering judgment on the floor of the House we decided that it would be a good idea for each of us to make a very short statement summarising, very unusually, it would be a very short statement, sort of three or four sentences explaining why we were reaching the decision we were. This certainly was directed to the public because we knew that this was going to be televised.

By using a form of content analysis, which adds a new dimension to the scholarly scrutiny of judicial pronouncements, it is possible to demonstrate the different flavour and emphasis of Lord Bingham's judgment in *Belmarsh* from those of some of his principal colleagues in the case (Figures 4.9, 4.10, 4.11 and 4.12. In Wordles size of words reflects frequency of use).

In *Belmarsh* Lord Bingham was engaging in a conscious dialogue with not only the Government but also the public. With the Executive Lord Bingham was steering a masterly course 'between the shoals of political deference and the reefs of judicial supremacism' as Stephen Sedley memorably put

Figure 4.9   Wordle: Lord Bingham, Belmarsh

Figure 4.10   Wordle: Lord Hoffmann, Belmarsh

Figure 4.11   Wordle: Lord Rodger, Belmarsh

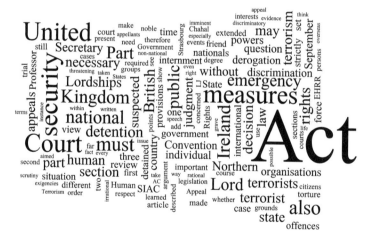

Figure 4.12   Wordle: Lord Walker, Belmarsh

it.[125] He wished to lay down clear parameters to the Executive's anti-terrorism powers, which inevitably took the courts into the political territory of publicly curbing the powers of the other two branches of government. Tom was well aware of the damage caused by highly publicised spats between Home Secretaries and the courts. He was also aware that judges were non-elected. Nevertheless, he had no truck with the Attorney General suggesting that judicial decision-making was in some way undemocratic and told him so. However, despite the provocation in the Attorney General's argument and in the prior challenge to Lord Steyn, Lord Bingham deliberately downplayed the rhetoric in order (successfully) to avoid the media headlines which in the recent past had soured relations between two branches of the state.[126] The House had handed the Executive a rebuff, but had done so in a manner that minimised the hurt.[127] As for the dialogue with the public, we know that Lord Bingham wanted the law and its institutions to be accessible to the populace. This was part of his first principle

[125] Stephen Sedley, 'The Long Sleep', in Andenas and Fairgrieve (eds.), *Tom Bingham and the Transformation of the Law* (2009), p. 183.

[126] Such headlines have emerged again with David Cameron's slightly intemperate remarks in February 2011 about the Supreme Court's ruling on the right of a sex offender to have their position on the Sex Offender's Register reviewed. See D. Pannick, 'The Prime Minister and the Home Secretary Should know Better', *The Times*, 24 February 2011.

[127] In so doing, Lord Bingham demonstrated the restraint that Vernon Bogdanor has declared to be necessary in order to maintain the compromise between parliamentary sovereignty and the rule of law which was enshrined in the Human Rights Act. See Bogdanor, *The New British Constitution*, p. 69.

of the Rule of Law,[128] because he saw it as essential for public respect for the law and the courts. What social scientists call the legitimacy issue. Lord Bingham knew that by eschewing rhetorical phrases he was making the dialogue with the public more difficult, since he was unsure that the public would make much of an intricate argument about derogation from the Convention. However, he knew that the public good required that the public should see that the judiciary were protecting the liberty of the individual citizen, even foreign nationals, and that especially in the aftermath of 9/11 the rule of law and fundamental human rights required that there be rational, proportionate and non-discriminatory limits to the Government's anti-terrorism powers. Miss Hamlyn would, I think, have approved.

[128] Bingham, *The Rule of Law*, p. 47.

5

Conclusion: where next?

In the earlier chapters I have argued that the public interest in relation to three key institutions in a democracy – lawyers, access to justice and the judiciary – is now a matter that is too important to be left to lawyers and judges alone to determine. Without doubt, dialogues with non-lawyer stakeholders are becoming more prevalent with respect to these institutions, and these stakeholders are increasingly making their voices heard wherever such determinations are being made.

As we have seen, the very concept of professionalism for lawyers has been re-negotiated over the last thirty years between the state, regulators and consumer bodies, on the one hand, and the profession, on the other, in order to redress a perceived failure to achieve a balance between professional obligations and professional benefits that was in the public interest. These dialogues have been particularly active in relation to the elements of market control, public protection and autonomy. For the first, consumer pressure (allied to that from the Office of Fair Trading[1] and, more recently, the Legal Services Board[2]) is introducing ever more competition – with

---

[1] Director General of Fair Trading, *Competition in the Professions* (London: Office of Fair Trading, 2001).
[2] C. Decker and G. Yarrow, *Understanding the Economic Rationale for Legal Services Regulation* (London: Regulatory Policy Institute, 2010) and Legal Service Board, *Understanding the Economic Rationale for Legal Services Regulation – A Collection of Essays* (London: Legal Services Board, 2011).

ABS being but the latest exemplar. As for public protection and autonomy, the dialogues with government, regulators and consumers have convinced the professional bodies that there must be a significant lay participation at all stages in the complaints process, from the new single gateways for complaints, to the panels of the disciplinary tribunals. Both in England and Scotland non-lawyers have begun to input to the drafting of new professional standards of conduct and service. Further, the movement away from self-regulation has led to lay stakeholders being on almost all regulatory bodies in connection with the legal profession in the United Kingdom, with a view to ensuring that the profession does not lose sight of the public good.

While politicians have been active in the access to justice debates in the United Kingdom in recent years – and especially in relation to legal aid cuts – so, too, have lay providers in the not-for-profit sector. Moreover, lay stakeholders representing the public interest in access to justice comprise the great bulk of the management committees of law centres in Scotland and England, and almost half of the Boards of the Legal Services Commission and of the Scottish Legal Aid Board. However, to date they have had less input into bodies that deal with the rules of court (including Mckenzie friends) or the setting of court fees.

With respect to the judiciary, direct dialogue[3] with politicians and government remains a fraught area, as we saw

---

[3] Indirect dialogue whereby the judges interpret legislation and (occasionally) Hansard is commonplace and relatively unproblematic, unless the Supreme Court is criticising the Executive or making a declaration of incompatibility with respect to the European Convention

in Chapter 4. Nevertheless, Charles Clarke MP has continued his campaign for greater dialogue between the Executive and judicial branches of government,[4] and the appearances of the Lord Chief Justice and the Lord Chancellor before the Constitutional Committee of the House of Lords suggest that this dialogue may grow. Even out and out lay stakeholders have been making progress in influencing public interest issues with respect to the judiciary. On the Court Services body that run the courts in Scotland there are now lay members. All of the bodies responsible for judicial appointments in the United Kingdom contain a significant group of lay members, and two of the three are chaired by a layperson. Judicial complaints and discipline also involves independent lay oversight.

However, the growing participation of laypersons in the determination of the public good with respect to these key institutions of the democratic process necessarily prompts further reflections. Is there sufficient opportunity for the public interest to express itself in the ruling councils of the profession, the judiciary and legal aid bodies?[5] Do we need to do more to enable a clearer expression of the interests of society to be voiced, untainted by professional interests and governmental economics? What is 'lay-ness' in this context? Is it

on Human Rights. Equally, where the Executive or Parliament comment on judicial decisions, the indirect dialogue can also grow tense (see fn. 11, Chapter 4 above).

[4] See the Foundation for Law, Justice and Society debate at Magdalen College, Oxford on the 'Role of Courts in a Democracy', 11 February 2011, available at: www.fljs.org/section.aspx?id=2946.

[5] See National Consumer Council, *Three Steps to Credible Self Regulation* (London: National Consumer Council, 2003).

simply not being a lawyer? Should non-lawyer system insiders, for example, those who work in the courts or access to justice field, be regarded as lay stakeholders in this context? Is a non-practising lawyer a lay person? We must be wary of the dangers of tokenism, but also of mistaking the colonisation of legal institutions by other professions as an infusion of 'layness'. Sometimes it is desirable that the lay input provides an expertise in areas that the lawyers lack, for example, managerialism, personnel, audit and accounts, education and training.[6] At other times, the desirable perspective is of a consumer of legal services, and those who deal with consumers on a regular basis are not always best placed to represent the views *of the consumer* with respect to legal services and access to justice. At other times, again, the role of the lay member is that of critical friend or watchdog: the hypothetical reasonable person or the independent, fair-minded, fully informed lay person.[7] Here legal academics can often play a valuable role, since they are neither fully lay nor fully lawyer. Having a foot in both camps can provide a bridge to mutual understanding between the lay and legal members of juristic bodies. Either way, at long last 'the Common people of this Country', as Miss Hamlyn put it, are beginning to play their rightful part in determining the public good when it comes to lawyers, access to justice and the judiciary. The challenge for all of us is to make that participation effective.

---

[6] For example, the Judicial Appointments Board for Scotland, or the Quality Assurance Committee of the Law Society of Scotland, which has oversight of its peer review programme.

[7] See, e.g., *Porter v. Magill* [2002] 1 All ER 465 at para. 103 *per* Lord Hope.

BIBLIOGRAPHY

Abel, R., *English Lawyers between Market and State* (Oxford University Press, 2003).

'The Decline of Professionalism', *Modern Law Review,* 49 (1986), 1.

American Bar Association, 'In the Spirit of Public Service,' Report of the Commission on Professionalism (Chicago, IL: American Bar Association, 1986).

Arthurs, H. W., 'The Dead Parrot: Does Professional Self-regulation Exhibit Vital Signs?', *Alberta Law Review,* 33 (1995), 800.

Australian Government, A Strategic Framework for Access to Justice in the Federal Civil Justice System: A Guide for Future Action, 2009, available at: www.ag.gov.au/a2j; www.ag.gov.au/www/agd/rwpattach.nsf.

Baker, L., *Brandeis and Frankfurter, A Dual Biography* (New York: Harper & Row, 1984).

Baksi, C., 'Neuberger Endorses Accreditation Scheme', *Law Society Gazette,* 10 November 2010.

'Where Will the Legal Aid Lawyers of the Future Come From?', *Law Society Gazette,* 28 October 2010.

Barak, A., *The Judge in a Democracy* (Princeton University Press, 2006).

Beaton, G., *Why Professionalism is still Relevant,* 2010, available at: au.linkedin.com/in/georgerbeaton.

Bellingham, H., 'Worth Fighting For', in Robins (ed.), *Closing the Justice Gap,* p. 14.

Bindman, G., 'No Substitute', in Robins (ed.), *Closing the Justice Gap,* p. 21.

'What Money could Buy', in J. Robins (ed.), *Pro Bono: Good Enough?* (London: Solicitors Journal, 2010), p. 11, available at:

www.solicitorsjournal.com/pictures/web/s/h/d/SJ%20Pro%20
Bono.pdf.

Bingham, Lord T., *The Rule of Law* (London: Allen Lane, 2010).
'The Rule of Law', *Cambridge Law Journal*, 66 (2007), 67–85.

Blom-Cooper, L. and Drewry, G., *Final Appeal* (Oxford: Clarendon Press, 1972).

Boffey, E., 'Raising the Bar: The Impact of Solicitor Advocates in Scotland'. Honours Dissertation, Strathclyde University Law School, 2010.

Bogdanor, V., *The New British Constitution* (Oxford: Hart Publishing, 2009).

Boon, A. *et al.*, 'Postmodern Professions?', *Journal of Law and Society*, 32 (2005), 473.

Boon, A. and Levin, J., *The Ethics and Conduct of Lawyers in England and Wales*, 2nd edn (Oxford: Hart Publishing, 2008).

Burke, E., adapted by George Santayana, *Reason in Common Sense*, vol. 1 (New York: Dover, 1980).

Canivet, G., Andenas, M. and Fairgrieve, D. (eds.), *Independence, Accountability and the Judiciary* (London: BIICL, 2006).

Cape, E. and Moorhead, R., 'Demand Induced Supply? A Report to the Legal Services Commission' (London: Legal Services Commission, 2005).

Cappelletti, M. and Garth, B. (eds.), *Access to Justice* (Amsterdam: Sitjoff & Noordhoff, 1978).

Carter, Lord D., Review, *Legal Aid, A Market-based Approach to Reform* (London: Department for Constitutional Affairs, 2006).

Cashman, P., 'Third Party Funding: A Changing Landscape', *Civil Justice Quarterly*, 27:3 (2008), 312–41.

Caulkin, S., 'Are the Real Pros being Managed out of Existence?', *The Observer*, June 2006.

Ciolino, D., 'Redefining Professionalism as Seeking', *Loyola Law Review*, 49 (2003), 229.

Clark, M., 'Introducing a Parliamentary Confirmation Process for New Supreme Court Justices', *Public Law* (2010), 464.

Clementi, D., *Review of the Regulatory Framework for Legal Services in England and Wales*, Final Report (London: Ministry of Justice, December 2004).

Coulehan, J., 'You say Self-interest, I say Altruism', in D. Wear *et al.* (eds.), *Professionalism in Medicine* (New York: Springer, 2006), p. 124.

Cownie, F. and Cocks, R., *A Great and Noble Occupation* (Oxford: Hart Publishing, 2009).

Dare, T., *The Counsel of Rogues? A Defence of the Standard Conception of the Lawyer's Role* (Aldershot: Ashgate, 2009).

Decker, C. and Yarrow, G., *Understanding the Economic Rationale for Legal Services Regulation* (London: Regulatory Policy Institute, 2010).

Dickson, B., 'The Processing of Appeals in the House of Lords', *Law Quarterly Review*, 123 (2007), 571–601.

Director General of Fair Trading, *Competition in the Professions* (London: Office of Fair Trading, 2001).

Edwards, H. T., 'The Effects of Collegiality on Judicial Decision-Making', *University of Pennsylvania Law Review*, 151 (2003), 1639.

European Commission for the Efficiency of Justice, *Fourth Evaluation Report on European Judicial Systems* (Strasbourg: Council of Europe, 2010).

Foundation for Law, Justice and Society, debate on the 'Role of Courts in a Democracy', Magdalen College, Oxford, 11 February 2011, available at: www.fljs.org/section.aspx?id=2946.

Galanter, M., 'Access to Justice in a World of Expanding Social Capability', *Fordham Urban Law Journal*, 37 (2010), 115.

　Lowering the Bar, Lawyer Jokes and Legal Culture (Madison, WI: University of Wisconsin Press, 2005).

'Why the "Haves" come out Ahead', *Law and Society Law Review*, 9 (1974), 95–160.

Garth, B., 'Rethinking the Legal Profession's Approach to Collective Self-Improvement: Competence and the Consumer Perspective', *Wisconsin Law Review*, (1983), 639.

Gearty, C., *Can Human Rights Survive?*, The Hamlyn Lectures, 57th Series (Cambridge University Press, 2006).

Genn, H., *Judging Civil Justice*, The Hamlyn Lectures, 60th Series (Cambridge University Press, 2008).

   Paths to Justice Scotland (Oxford: Hart Publishing, 2001).

   Paths to Justice (Oxford: Hart Publishing, 1999).

Gibb, F., 'Supreme Ambition, Jealousy and Outrage', *The Times*, 4 February 2010.

   'Judges Oppose Appointment of Sumption QC to the Supreme Court', *The Times*, 15 October 2009.

Gill, B., *Scottish Civil Courts Review*, 2009, available at: www.scotcourts.gov.uk/civilcourtsreview/theReport/Vol1Chap1_9.pdf.

Glasser, C., 'The Legal Profession in the 1990s', *Legal Studies*, 10 (1990), 1.

Goriely, T., 'Civil Legal Aid in England and Wales 1914 to 1961: the Emergence of a Paid Scheme', unpublished Ph.D. thesis, University College, London, 2003.

Goriely, T. and Paterson, A., 'Resourcing Civil Justice', in Paterson and Goriely (eds.), *Resourcing Civil Justice*, pp. 1–35.

Goriely, T., 'Rushcliffe 50 Years On', in Paterson and Goriely (eds.), *Resourcing Civil Justice*, p. 221.

Griffith, J., 'The Brave New World of Sir John Laws', *Modern Law Review*, 63 (2000), 159.

Griffiths, J., 'The Distribution of Legal Services in the Netherlands', *British Journal of Law and Society* 4 (1977), 282.

Hafferty, F., 'Measuring Professionalism: A Commentary', in Stern, D. (ed.), *Measuring Medical Professionalism* (Oxford University Press, 2006), p. 281.

Hale, Lady B., 'A Supreme Judicial Leader', in M. Andenas and D. Fairgrieve (eds.), *Tom Bingham and the Transformation of the Law* (Oxford University Press, 2009), p. 219.

'Equality and the Judiciary: Why Should we Want More Women Judges?', *Public Law* (2001), 489.

Hammond, G., *Judicial Recusal* (Oxford: Hart Publishing, 2009).

Hand, J., 'The Compensation Culture', *Journal of Law and Society*, 37 (2010), 569.

Hanlon, G., *Lawyers, the State and the Market* (London: Macmillan, 1990).

Harvey, T. and Munro, C., *Thalidomide: The Legal Aftermath* (Farnborough: Saxon House, 1976).

Hough, B., 'Access to Justice by Investing in Courts', unpublished paper, International Legal Aid Group conference, Wellington, New Zealand, 3 April 2009, available at: www.ilagnet.org/papers.php.

Hunt, P., *Legal Services Regulation Review* (London: Law Society, 2009).

Hurlburt, W. H., *The Self-Regulation of the Legal Profession in Canada and in England and Wales* (Edmonton: Alberta, Law Society of Alberta and Alberta Law Reform Institute, 2000).

Hynes, S., 'Publicly Funded Legal Advice gets a Ringing Endorsement', *Law Society Gazette*, 11 November 2010.

Hynes, S. and Robins, J., *The Justice Gap* (London: Legal Action Group, 2009).

Irvine, Lord, *Modernising Justice*, Cm. 4155 (London: Lord Chancellor's Department, 1998).

Jackson, Lord R., *Review of Civil Litigation Costs: Final Report* (London: Ministry of Justice, 2010), available at: www.judiciary.gov.uk/Resources/JCO/Documents/jackson-final-report-140110.pdf.

Janes, L., 'What are Legal Aid Lawyers For?', in Robins (ed.), *Closing the Justice Gap*, p. 32.

Kafka, F., *The Trial* (London: Penguin Books, 1994).

Kenny, C., 'The Paradoxes of Regulatory Reform', Oxford/Harvard Legal Symposium, 11 September 2009, p. 8. See LSB website at: www.legalservicesboard.org.uk.

Kilian, M., 'Legal Expenses Insurances: Preconditions, Pitfalls and Challenges', unpublished conference paper, Research into Practice: Legal Services Delivery in a New Decade, LSRC Legal Aid Conference, Cambridge, 2010.

Kinsella, N., 'Evolution Not Revolution', in Robins (ed.), *Closing the Justice Gap*, p. 43.

Kritzer, H., 'The Professions are Dead, Long live the Professions: Legal Practice in a Post Professional World' *Law and Society Review*, 33 (1999), 713.

Kronman, A., *The Lost Lawyer* (Cambridge, MA: Harvard University Press, 1993).

Law Society of England and Wales, Response to the Legal Aid Reform Consultation Paper, *Green Paper Proposals for the Reform of Legal Aid in England and Wales* (London: Law Society, February 2011), available at: www.justice.gov.uk/consultations/legal-aid-reform-151110.htm.

Access to Justice Review (London: Law Society, 2010).

Lee, J., 'A Defence of Concurring Speeches', *Public Law* (2009), 305.

Legal Action Group, 'Accounting for Overpayments', *Legal Action*, January 2011, 3.

Legal Services Board, *Understanding the Economic Rationale for Legal Services Regulation – A Collection Of Essays* (London: Legal Services Board, 2011).

'Referral Fees, Referral Arrangements and Fee Sharing', Discussion Document (London: Legal Services Board, September 2010), para. 1.13, available at: www.legalservicesboard.org.uk/what_we_do/pdf/20100929_referral_fees.pdf.

Legal Services Commission, 'Quality Assurance for Advocates', Discussion Paper, February 2010, available at: www.legalservices. gov.uk/docs/cds_main/QAADiscussionPaper_Feb2010.pdf.

Legal Services Consumer Panel, *Quality in Legal Services* (London: Legal Services Consumer Panel, November 2010).

Legal Services Institute, *The Regulation of Legal Services* (London: College of Law, February 2011).

Legal Services Ombudsman, *Annual Report, 2001–2002* (London: Stationery Office, 2002).

Legg, T., 'Judges for the New Century', *Public Law* (2001), 62.

Le Sueur, A., 'Developing Mechanisms for Judicial Accountability in the UK', *Legal Studies,* 24 (2004), 73.

Liptak, A., 'Justices are Long on Words but Short on Guidance', *New York Times,* 17 November 2010.

Loughrey, J., *Corporate Lawyers and Corporate Governance: International Corporate Law and Financial Market Regulation* (Cambridge University Press, 2011).

Lukes, S., *Power: A Radical View*, 2nd edn (Basingstoke: Palgrave Macmillan, 2005).

Mackay, Lord J., 'Legal aid Targeting Need', Cm. 2854 (London: Lord Chancellor's Department, 1995).

Macqueen, H. 2010. 'Scotland's First Female Law Graduates', available at: http://womeninlaw.law.ed.ac.uk/documents/WilsonLecture.pdf.

Magee, I., *Review of Legal Aid Delivery and Governance* (London: Ministry of Justice, 2010), available at: www.justice.gov.uk/publications/docs/legal-aid-delivery.pdf.

Malleson, K., 'Is the Supreme Court a Constitutional Court in all but Name?', paper delivered at conference on 'The Supreme Court and the Constitution', Queen Mary University of London, 3 November 2010.

'Rethinking the Merit Principle in Judicial Selection', *Journal of Law and Society,* 33 (2006), 126–40.

'Selecting Judges in the Era of Devolution and Human Rights', in A. Le Sueur (ed.), *Building the UK's New Supreme Court* (Oxford University Press, 2004), p. 310.

Mansfield, M., 'A Fresh Vision', in Robins (ed.), *Closing the Justice Gap*, p. 8.

Markovits, D., *A Modern Legal Ethics* (Princeton University Press, 2010).

Marks, S., 'Views from an Australian Regulator', *Journal of the Professional Lawyer* (2009), 45.

McBride, J., 'Access to Justice and Human Rights Treaties', *Civil Justice Quarterly,* 17 (1998), 235–71.

Ministry of Justice, *Report of the Advisory Panel on Judicial Diversity* (London: Ministry of Justice, 2010).

Proposals for the Reform of Legal Aid in England and Wales, Consultation Paper, November, CP12/10, Cm 7967 (London: HMSO, 2010).

Study of Legal Advice and the Local Level (London: Ministry of Justice, 1999).

Transforming the Legal Aid System (Wellington: Ministry of Justice, 2009).

Moorhead, R., 'Legal Aid – System Failure or Broken Law?', *New Law Journal,* March (2010), 403.

Community Legal Advice Centres and Networks: A Process Evaluation (London: Legal Services Research Centre, 2010).

'Lawyer Specialisation – Managing the Professional Paradox', *Law and Policy,* 32 (2010), 226.

Lawyer Watch, 'Litigants in Person: What the Research Really Says', posted on 16 December 2010, available at: http://lawyer-watch.wordpress.com/2010/12/16.

Pioneers in Practice: The Community Legal Service Pioneer Partnership Research Project (London: Lord Chancellor's Department, 2000).

Murray, L., *The Pleader* (Edinburgh: Mainstream Publishing, 2002).

National Audit Office, *Report of the Comptroller and Auditor General to the Houses of Parliament on the Community Legal Service Fund and the Criminal Defence Service accounts for the year ended 31 March 2010* (London: The Stationery Office, 2010).

The Procurement of Criminal Legal Aid in England and Wales by the Legal Services Commission, 27 November 2009 (London: The Stationery Office, 2009).

National Consumer Council, *Three Steps to Credible Self Regulation* (London: National Consumer Council, 2003).

Nelson, R. *et al.*, *Lawyers' Ideals/Lawyers' Practices: Transformations in the American Legal Profession* (New York: Cornell University Press, 1992).

Neuberger, Lord D., 'Swindlers (including the Master of the Rolls?) Not Wanted: Bentham and Justice Reform', Bentham Lecture, UCL Laws Bentham Association Dinner, March 2011.

Nicolson, D. and Webb, J., *Professional Legal Ethics* (Oxford University Press, 1999).

Ogus, A., *Regulation: Legal Form and Economic Theory* (Oxford: Hart Publishing, 2004).

Oliver, D. (ed.), *Justice, Legality and the Rule of Law* (Oxford University Press, 2009).

Panel on Fair Access to the Professions, *Unleashing Aspiration* (London: Institute of Career Guidance, Cabinet Office, 2009), available at: www.icg-uk.org/article607.html.

Pannick, Lord D., 'The Prime Minister and the Home Secretary Should know Better', *The Times*, 24 February 2011.

'The High Price to be Paid if Judges Examine our Historical Events', *The Times*, 17 June 2010.

Parker, C., *Just Lawyers* (Oxford University Press, 1999).

'Law Deregulation via Business Deregulation', *International Journal of the Legal Profession*, 6 (1999), 175.

'Competing Images of the Legal Profession: Competing Regulatory Strategies', *International Journal of the Sociology of Law* 25 (1997), 385.

Passmore, C., 'The Future is Bright', in Robins (ed.), *Closing the Justice Gap*, pp. 25–9.

Paterson, A., 'Does Advocacy Matter in the Lords?', in J. Lee (ed.), *From House of Lords to Supreme Court* (Oxford: Hart Publishing, 2011), ch. 12.

'The Scottish Judicial Appointments Board: New Wine in Old Bottles', in P. Russell and K. Malleson (eds.), *Appointing Judges in an Age of Judicial Power* (University of Toronto Press, 2006), ch. 1.

'Self-Regulation and the Future of the Profession', in D. Hayton (ed.), *Law's Future* (Oxford: Hart Publishing, 2000).

'Professionalism and the Legal Services Market', *International Journal of Legal Studies* 3 (1996), 137.

'Scottish Lords of Appeal 1876–1988', *The Juridical Review* (1988), 235.

The Law Lords (London: Macmillan, 1982).

Paterson, A. and Goriely, T. (eds.), *Resourcing Civil Justice* (Oxford University Press, 1996).

Paterson, A. and Ritchie, B., *Law, Practice and Conduct for Solicitors* (Edinburgh: W. Green, 2006), ch. 10.

Pearce, R., 'How Law Firms can do Good while Doing Well (and the Answer is Not Pro Bono)', *Fordham Urban Law Journal, Symposium on Professional Challenges in Large-Firm Practice*, 33 (2005), 221.

'The Professionalism Paradigm Shift', *New York University Law Review*, 70 (1995), 1229.

Peresie, J., 'Female Judges Matter', *Yale Law Journal*, 114 (2005), 1759.

Philippsohn, S. and Mascarenhas, T., 'A Class Apart', *European Law*, 87 (2009), 14.

Phillips, Lord N., 'Introductory Tribute: Lord Bingham of Cornhill', in M. Andenas and D. Fairgrieve (eds.), *Tom Bingham and the Transformation of the Law* (Oxford University Press, 2009), p. xlix.

Pleasence, P., *Causes of Action*, 2nd edn (London: The Stationery Office, 2006).

Reshaping Medical Workforce Project Board, *Consultation on Speciality Training Numbers from 2011 to 2015* (Edinburgh: Scottish Executive, 2010).

Rhode, D., 'Professionalism', *South Carolina Law Review*, 52 (2001), 459.

'The Professionalism Problem', *William & Mary Law Review* 39 (1998), 283.

'Policing the Professional Monopoly', *Stanford Law Review* 34 (1981), 1.

Robins, J. (ed.), *Closing the Justice Gap* (London: Solicitors Journal, 2010), available at: www.solicitorsjournal.com/Pictures/Web/k/l/p/Closing%20the%20Justice%20Gap.pdf.

Rosen, R. and Dewar, S., 'On Being a Doctor', A King's Fund Discussion Paper (London, 2004).

Ross, Y., *The Jokes on Lawyers* (Sydney: Federation Press, 1996).

Rothwell, R., 'Increase Alcohol Tax to Fund Legal Aid, says Law Society', *Law Society Gazette*, 15 November 2010.

Royal Commission on Legal Services in Scotland, Cmnd 7846 (Edinburgh: HMSO, 1980).

Sandefur, R., 'The Fulcrum point of Equal Access to Justice', *Loyola of Los Angeles Law Review* 42 (2009), 949.

Scottish Executive, *Report by the Research Working Group on Competition in the Legal Services Market in Scotland* (Edinburgh: Scottish Executive, 2006).

Review of Legal Information and Advice Provision (Edinburgh: Scottish Executive, 2001).

Scottish Legal News, 'Tougher Legal Funding over next 5 years', 24 November 2010.

Sedley, S., 'The Long Sleep', in M. Andenas and D. Fairgrieve (eds.), *Tom Bingham and the Transformation of the Law* (Oxford University Press, 2009), p. 183.

Seneviratne, M., *The Legal Profession: Regulation and the Consumer* (London: Sweet & Maxwell, 1999).

Sellar, W. C. and Yeatman, R. J., *1066 and All That* (London: Methuen, 1930).

Sherr, A. and Paterson, A., 'Professional Competence, Peer Review and Quality Assurance in England and Wales and in Scotland', *Alberta Law Review*, 45 (2008), 151.

Sherr, A., Paterson, A. and Moorhead, R., *Lawyers the Quality Agenda* (London: HMSO, 1994).

Simms, A. *et al.*, *Ghost Town Britain, the Threat from Economic Globalisation to Livelihoods, Liberty and Local Economic Reform* (London, The New Economics Foundation, 2002).

Smith, R., 'Justice', *ILAG Newsletter*, March/April 2010.

'The Justice Gap: Whatever Happened to Legal Aid?', *New Law Journal* 159 (2009), 866.

'Special Delivery', in Robins (ed.), *Closing the Justice Gap*, p. 16.

Solicitors Regulatory Agency, *Achieving the Right Outcomes*. Redditch, January 2010.

Sommerlad, H., 'Managerialism and the Legal Profession', *International Journal of the Legal Profession*, 2 (1995), 159.

SPADA, *British Professions Today: the State of the Sector* (London: SPADA, 2009).

Stephen, F., *Legal Aid Expenditure in Scotland* (Edinburgh: Law Society, 1999).

Stevens, R. B., 'Reform in Haste and Repent at Leisure', *Legal Studies*, 24 (2004), 1.

   The English Judges (Oxford: Hart Publishing, 2002).

   'Unpacking the Judges', *Current Legal Problems*, 1 (1993), 2.

   'The Role of a Final Appeal Court in a Democracy', *Modern Law Review*, 28 (1965), 509.

Stevenson, R. L., *Edinburgh: Picturesque Notes* (Edinburgh, 1897).

Steyn, J., 'Guantanamo Bay: The Legal Black Hole', 27th FA Mann Lecture, 25 November 2003.

Sturgess, G. and Chubb, P., *Judging the World* (Sydney: Butterworths, 1988).

Susskind, R., *The End of Lawyers?* (Oxford University Press, 2008, paperback edn 2010).

The Scottish Office, *Access to Justice: Beyond the Year 2000* (Edinburgh: The Scottish Office, 1998).

Thomson Review: Rights of Audience in the Supreme Courts in Scotland (Edinburgh: Scottish Executive, April 2011), available at: www.scotland.gov.uk/Publications/2010/03/15112328/0.

Todd, P., 'Declining Popularity', in Robins (ed.), *Closing the Justice Gap*, p. 59.

Tomkins, A., 'National Security and the Role of the Court: A Changed Landscape?', *Law Quarterly Review*, 126 (2010), 543–67.

Trigg, J., 'Citizen Power', in Robins (ed.), *Closing the Justice Gap*, p. 53.

Wear, D. and Aultman, J. (eds.), *Professionalism in Medicine: Critical Perspectives* (New York: Springer, 2006).

Wright, T. *et al.*, 'The Common Law of Contracts: Are Broad Principles Better than Detailed Rules? An Empirical Investigation', *Texas Wesleyan Law Review* 11 (2005), 399–420.

Young, Lord D., *Common Sense, Common Safety* (London: Cabinet Office, October 2010).

Zander, M., *The State of Justice*, The Hamlyn Lectures, 51st Series (London: Sweet & Maxwell, 1999).

Legal Services for the Community (London: Temple Smith, 1978).

Lawyers and the Public Interest (London: Weidenfeld and Nicolson, 1968).

INDEX

INDEX